The Greek Library of Saints John and Paul
(San Zanipolo) at Venice

MEDIEVAL AND RENAISSANCE
TEXTS AND STUDIES
VOLUME 391

The Greek Library of Saints John and Paul (San Zanipolo) at Venice

Donald F. Jackson

ACMRS
(Arizona Center for Medieval and Renaissance Studies)
Tempe, Arizona
2011

Published by ACMRS (Arizona Center for Medieval and Renaissance Studies)
Tempe, Arizona
© 2011 by the Arizona Board of Regents for Arizona State University
All Rights Reserved

Library of Congress Cataloging-in-Publication Data

Jackson, Donald F.
 The Greek library of Saints John and Paul (San Zanipolo) at Venice / Donald F. Jackson.
   p. cm. -- (Medieval and Renaissance texts and studies ; v. 391)
 Includes bibliographical references and index.
 ISBN 978-0-86698-439-3 (alk. paper)
 1. Manuscripts, Greek--Italy--Venice--Catalogs. 2. Manuscripts, Greek (Medieval and modern)--Italy--Venice--Catalogs. 3. San Giovanni e Paolo (Church : Venice, Italy). Biblioteca--Catalogs. 4. Biblioteca nazionale marciana --Catalogs. I. Title.
  Z6605.G7J33 2011
  015.045'31131--dc23

2011028957

∞
This book is made to last. It is set in Adobe Caslon Pro,
smyth-sewn and printed on acid-free paper to library specifications.
Printed in the United States of America

Table of Contents

Introduction	*vii*
Chapter I: Janus Lascaris and Gioachino Torriano	1
Chapter II: Marcon's B List	7
Chapter III: Marcon's A List	25
Chapter IV: Gioachino Torriano's Grand Plan	37
Chapter V: The *Pulcherrimi* and Marcus Musurus	43
Chapter VI: Martin Richter's List	49
Chapter VII: Conrad Gesner and San Zanipolo	57
Chapter VIII: Girolamo Vielmi and the Zanipolo Library	61
Chapter IX: The Tomasini List	67
Zanipolo Manuscripts Acquired Late	73
Concordance of Manuscript References	75
Index of Greek Authors and Subjects	79
Appendix I	83
Appendix II	91

Introduction

Early in the sixteenth century the library of the Dominican community in the parish and school of the church of Saints John and Paul at Venice reached its greatest size and excellence. Venice was not yet the center for scholarly research that it was soon to become. The city owned the magnificent collection of Greek manuscripts accumulated by the expatriate Orthodox prelate who became the Roman Cardinal Bessarion. But this collection was packed away in cases behind a partition in the Palace of the Doges and available for limited use to only a few favored scholars.[1] Long before these manuscripts became available to the public for admiration and study, as promised the Cardinal by the Venetian Senate, Zanipolo drew scholars from all over Italy and northern Europe.[2] Only in 1523 did San Zanipolo acquire a rival in Venice, a library and reading room created by Cardinal Domenico Grimani for his Greek, Latin, and Hebrew manuscripts, at S. Antonio di Castello.[3]

By 1523 the collection at San Zanipolo was beginning to be dispersed. The library had thrived under the direction of Gioachino Torriano, the community's superior for a time and later a Governor General of the Dominican Order, who died in 1500.[4] His passion for book collecting appears to have been shared by

---

[1] For more on the Bessarion collection. see Lotte Labowsky, *Bessarion's Library and the Biblioteca Marciana* (Rome, 1979); M.J.C. Lowry, "Two Great Venetian Libraries in the Age of Aldus Manutius," *Bulletin of the John Rylands Library* 57 (1974): 128–66; Marino Zorzi, "Bessarione e i codici greci," in *L'eredità greca e l'ellenismo veneziano*, ed. G. Benzoni (Venice, 2002); 93–121.

[2] For a good presentation of the various private and monastic libraries at Venice in the sixteenth century see Marino Zorzi, "La circolazione del libro a Venezia nel cinquecento: Biblioteche private e pubbliche," *Ateneo Veneto* 177 (1990): 117–89.

[3] See Lowry, "Two Great Venetian Libraries," and Theobald Freudenberger, "Die Bibliothek des Kardinals Domenico Grimani," *Historisches Jahrbuch* 56 (1936): 15–45. For the fate of this collection and a good description of its genesis see A. Diller, H.D. Saffrey, and L.G. Westerink, *Bibliotheca Graeca Manuscripta Cardinalis Dominici Grimani (1461–1523)*, Bibliotheca Nazionale Marciana Collana di Studi 1 (Venice, 2004). See also the excellent review by Davide Muratore, *Medioevo greco* 4 (2004): 256–73.

[4] See Susy Marcon, "Per la biblioteca a stampa del domenicano Gioachino Torriano," *Miscellanea marciana* 1 (1986): 223–48. Marcon presents a fine overview of Torriano's religious and professional life (esp. 220–25), as well as a thorough listing of bibliographical material.

no surviving members of the community. Loss of books began soon after his death and continued through the century, but the period of greatest loss seems to have occurred immediately after the middle of the sixteenth century, when many Zanipolo volumes were offered for sale by Andreas Darmarius and Nicolaus della Torre.[5] When Francesco Sansovino published in 1580 his great description of the city of Venice, the library at Saints John and Paul was a mediocre monastic collection worthy of little note, like other Venetian repositories then inferior to the great collection in the Marciana.[6]

While the overall collection continued to suffer losses in the seventeenth and eighteenth centuries, few Greek manuscripts were lost. When D. M. Berardelli prepared his excellent catalogue of the Zanipolo manuscripts, he found that several had been stolen "ab homine nequam, qui eorum pretium certe non ignorabat, & tempus opportunum pro huiusmodi sacrilego furto exequendo novit invenire."[7] But the list of lost volumes he provides includes only a few Greek authors, and these are in printed editions. Rinaldo Fulin, who has studied eighteenth-century losses in detail, finds that several Greek manuscripts were indeed removed from the library, but all were later returned.[8] The present study will show that a few Greek works were added to the collection after the decline of the library began. As far as the Greek manuscript collection of San Zanipolo is concerned, then, these additions constitute the only changes that can be documented between

---

[5] See D. F. Jackson, "The Greek Manuscripts of Jean Hurault de Boistaillé," *Studi italiani di filologia classica*, ser. 4, 2 (2004): 209–52; and, for the years before the arrival of Hurault in Venice, see Jean Irigoin, "Les ambassadeurs à Vénise et la commerce des manuscrits grecs dans les années 1540–1550, " in *Venezia: Centro di mediazione tra oriente e occidente (secoli XV–XVI)* (Florence, 1977), 2:399–415.

[6] I have used the edition of 1663: Fr. Sansovino, *Venetia, città nobilissima et singolare*, with additions by Marin Tiepolo (Farnborough, 1968). For more on the later history of San Zanipolo see M. Zorzi, "Le vicende delle biblioteche veneziane e la libreria dei SS. Giovanni e Paolo," in *La scuola grande di S. Marco, i saperi e l'arte*, ed. N.-E. Vanzan Marchini (Canova, 2001), 79–96.

[7] D.M. Berardelli, "Codicum omnium Graecorum, Arabicorum, aliarumque linguarum Orientalium qui manuscripti in Bibliotheca SS. Johannis et Pauli Venetiarum Ordinis Praedicatorum asservantur catalogus," in *Nuova raccolta d'opusculi scientifici e filologici* 20 (1770). This Greek inventory was soon followed by "Codicum omnium Latinorum & Italicorum qui manuscripti in Bibliotheca SS. Joannis et Pauli Venetiarum apud PP. Praedicatores asservantur catalogus," in the same journal, volumes 32 (1778), 33 (1779), 35 (1780), 37 (1782), 38 (1783), 39 (1784), and 40 (1784). Berardelli's note quoted above and his list of losses occur in his prefatory remarks to volume 33.

[8] R. Fulin, "Vicende della libreria in SS. Gio. e Paolo," *Ateneo Veneto*, ser. 2, 5 (1868): 273–94, especially 280–89. He also cites the instance, outside his own discoveries, of a Greek menologion which was sold by a Venetian bookseller (281–82).

1600 and 1789, when the city of Venice decided to transfer the remains of a once wonderful collection to the Marciana.[9]

In his catalogue of the Greek Appendix of the Biblioteca Marciana Elpidio Mioni has identified many manuscripts which formerly belonged to the Dominican community.[10] Mioni was helped in his identifications by the Berardelli catalogue of the Zanipolo collection which provided detailed descriptions of the Greek volumes at Zanipolo a few years before transfer of the collection to the Marciana. Many of the codices were taken to Paris during the Napoleonic wars, but almost all were returned. In the years since publication of Berardelli's catalogue losses from the collection have been minimal.

What follows here is an attempt to determine the origins of this once important collection of Greek manuscripts and to describe its size and quality before the losses noted above began. The reconstruction is based upon information from various published and unpublished sources: observations by visitors to the collection like Janus Lascaris, Martin Richter, Conrad Gesner, and Filippo Tomasini, as well as Torriano's own inventory and a supplement by the Dominican Giovanni de Rachaneto. Many of the manuscripts which departed from Zanipolo still exist and can be identified in other collections today. Identification leads to interesting and informative observations on the ultimate plan of Gioachino Torriano for the library at Saints John and Paul and the manuscripts of Cardinal Bessarion. A concluding section addresses some misinterpretations of Marcus Musurus' association with several Greek manuscripts in the collection, as well as dates and purpose for the construction of these volumes.

---

[9] The one exception to this statement is a Plato manuscript listed by Tomasini below.

[10] *Bibliothecae Divi Marci Venetiarum Codices Graeci Manuscripti*, ed. E. Mioni, Vol. 1: *Codices in classe A prima usque ad quintam inclusi, Pars prior* (Rome, 1967), XXVII.

I. Janus Lascaris and Gioachino Torriano

After the fall of Constantinople in 1453 Janus Lascaris and his family made their way into Italy, apparently by the route many other Greeks followed through those areas of Hellas which were successively swallowed up by the Turks. As a young man, probably around 1465, Lascaris studied at Padua and eventually became a member of the learned circle around Lorenzo de' Medici at Florence.[1] He taught in the Florentine Studio which had introduced Greek studies into the West early in the fifteenth century. By 1490 Lascaris had become chief hunter of Greek texts for Lorenzo. *Il Magnifico* had tried throughout the 1480s to purchase manuscript collections of deceased humanists and to create a family library which would complement the public collection at San Marco of Florence fostered by his grandfather, Cosimo the Elder, built upon the collection of Niccolò Niccoli.[2] His efforts at buying a library, except for the acquisition of many books of the famed educator Francesco Filelfo, were notably unsuccessful. Lorenzo therefore set about exploiting the services as scribes of Greek scholars in his circle and sending Lascaris out to locate authors and works not known at Florence.[3] His task was to buy any books available for sale and to note the location of others for later copying. He returned from the East in the autumn of 1492 with a large number of texts, only to find that Lorenzo had died in the spring.[4] Family fortunes failed in the next few years; the Medici went into exile and their library was left behind in Florence. But Lascaris' efforts in developing the family

---

[1] See B. Knos, *Un ambassadeur de l'hellénisme: Janus Lascari* (Paris, 1945).

[2] For the library at S. Marco of Florence see B.L. Ullman and P.A. Stadter, *The Public Library of Renaissance Florence* (Padua, 1972).

[3] For Filelfo's relations with Lorenzo see Diana Robin, *Filelfo in Milan* (Princeton, 1991), 10, 142. For documents related to Lascaris' activity in the East see E.S. Piccolomini, "Delle condizioni e delle vicende della libreria Medicea privata," *Archivio storico italiano* 19 (1874): 101–29, 254–81, 538–39; 21 (1875): 102–12, 282–96; idem, "Due documenti relativi ad acquisti di codici greci, fatti da G. Lascaris per conto di Lorenzo de' Medici," *Rivista italiana di filologia classica* 2 (1874): 401–23; 3 (1875): 150–52. See also the excellent study of Lascaris' journeys by Sebastiano Gentile, "Lorenzo e Giano Lascaris," in *Lorenzo il Magnifico e il suo mondo: Convegno internazionale di Studi, Firenze 9–13 Giugno 1992*, ed. G.C. Garfagnini (Florence, 1994), 177–94.

[4] See D. F. Jackson, "A New Look at an Old Book List," *Studi italiani di filologia classica*, ser. 3, 16 (1998): 83–108.

collection were lasting. Early in the sixteenth century Cardinal Giovanni de' Medici, Lorenzo's second son and eventually Pope Leo X, bought the library back from the community of San Marco of Florence.[5] Later in the century it became the nucleus of the modern Biblioteca Laurenziana.

When Lascaris set out for the East by way of Venice on his last hunt for Lorenzo, he visited several Italian collections along the way. He brought along a list of *desiderata*, works known at Florence only by reputation. These lists, as well as Lascaris' discoveries of desirable manuscripts in various places, are today preserved in cod. Vaticanus gr. 1412.[6] At one point in his diary Lascaris reported consecutively on Venetian collectors: Giorgio Valla, Gioachino Torriano, Alessandro Benedetti, and Ermolao Barbaro.[7] He thereby gives us a first look at the collection of Torriano:

παρὰ τῷ αἰδεσίμῳ Ἰωκείνῳ γενεράλ.

1. Ἀκτουαρίου προβλήματα ἰατρικά = Parisinus gr. 2153, fols. 290r–end. This is a composite codex. All of its parts may well have belonged to Torriano when Lascaris visited him, but only Actuarius caught his eye. All parts were at Zanipolo around 1500 (see Marcon A99 below). The composite codex in its present form came into the French royal collection among the manuscripts of Jean Hurault de Boistaillé in 1622.[8]
2. ἄθροισις εὐσύνοπτος τῶν μαθηματικῶν. At first glance this would appear to be a collection of mathematical writers. But there is no clear evidence of

---

[5] For the history of these events and an inventory of the Cardinal's library shortly before his election to the papacy see Piccolomini, "Libreria Medicea" and "Acquisti di codici greci", and E.B. Fryde, *Greek Manuscripts of the Private Library of the Medici 1469–1510* (Aberystwyth, 1996).

[6] All of Lascaris' notes contained in the Vatican manuscript were published by K.K. Mueller, "Neue Mittheilungen ueber Janos Laskaris und die Mediceische Bibliothek," *Zentralblatt fuer Bibliothekswesen* 1 (1884): 333–412. The *desiderata* begin on 367, notes for trips on 379. Further references in my discussion are made by citing folios in the manuscript as reported by Mueller.

[7] See Mueller, "Mittheilungen," 382–88. The bibliography on Valla, most of whose Greek manuscripts are now in Modena, and Barbaro is prodigious. As a sample see J.L. Heiberg, *Beitraege zur Geschichte G. Valla und seiner Bibliothek* (Leipzig, 1896); D. Fava, *La biblioteca estense nel suo sviluppo storico* (Modena, 1925); S. Bernardinello, *Autografi greci* (Padua, 1979), tav. 42; P. Rose, "Humanist Culture and Renaissance Mathematics: The Italian Libraries of the Quattrocento," *Studies in the Renaissance* 20 (1973): 46–105, here 94–100. For Barbaro manuscripts see A. Diller, "The Library of Francesco and Ermolao Barbaro," *Italia medioevale e umanistica* 6 (1963): 252–62; V. Branca, "L'umanesimo veneziano alla fine del quattrocento: Ermolao Barbaro e il suo circolo," in *Storia della cultura veneta*, vol. 3.1 (Vicenza, 1980), 123–75.

[8] For Hurault de Boistaillé see Jackson, "Greek Manuscripts."

such a text ever at San Zanipolo (see Richter 25 for an apparent mathematical text, now lost). Gesner, while discussing Pappus on Ptolemy's *Almagest*, says: "Invenio et hunc titulum voluminis in Italia (Zanipolo?) extantis, nescio an eiusdem cum iam dicto: συναγωγῆς μαθηματικῆς βιβ. 1."[9] If we can take συναγωγή as equivalent to ἄθροισις εὐσύνοπτος, Lascaris may well have been looking at Marcon B52 below.

3. Ἀλεξάνδρου εἰς τὰ μετεωρολογικὰ βιβλία δ´ = Marc. IV, 6 written by John Argyropulus. See B41 below.
4. Συμπλικίου εἰς τὰ τέσσαρα περὶ οὐρανοῦ = Parisinus gr. 1910. Dieter Harlfinger[10] has reported seeing the hand of John Argyropulus in margins here. The manuscript entered the French royal collection with the books of Colbert, having been acquired by him from Chandelier in 1674. See B 58 below.
5. Συμπλικίου εἰς τὸ περὶ ψυχῆς = Marc. IV, 19 written by John Argyropulus. See B42 below.
6. Θεμιστίου εἰς τὸ περὶ ψυχῆς = Marc. IV, 13 written by John Argyropulus. See B43 below.
7. σύνοψις τῆς λογικῆς ἁπάσης τοῦ Ἀριστοτέλους, οὗ ἡ ἀρχή σκοπὸς ἡμῖν ἐστιν θεοῦ συνάρσει = Marc. IV, 24. Discussed below at B47–48.
8. τοῦ Φιλοπόνου εἰς τὰ δ´ τῶν φυσικῶν = Marc. IV, 20. See B40 below.

Almost all of these items that Lascaris saw and deemed worthy of note when he visited Torriano come from one section of Torriano's own inventory (Marcon's B list below) which consists largely of acquisitions from John Argyropulus. More will be said about this group when the B list is treated in detail. For now it will suffice to deal with a few questions prompted by Lascaris' short list.

1. Does Lascaris' list tell us anything about the size of Torriano's collection in 1491? It does. Argyropulus had died at Rome four years earlier. His manuscripts were sold, some before he died, all by 1491. Giovanni Mercati has called attention to the fact that the Vatican Library purchased twelve manuscripts from Argyropulus between 1481 and 1484.[11] Deno Geanokoplos cites a letter of Constantine Lascaris saying that Argyropulus sold his books late in life so as to be able to buy food.[12] Torriano therefore acquired Argyropulus' volumes at least a

---

[9] Conrad Gesner, *Bibliotheca universalis* (Tiguri, 1545), vol. 1, fol. 535r.

[10] D. Harlfinger, *Textgeschichte der pseudo-aristotelischen Schrift ΠΕΡΙ ΑΤΟΜΩΝ ΓΡΑΜΜΩΝ* (Amsterdam, 1971), 408.

[11] G. Mercati, "Alcune aggiunte alla Ἀργυροπούλεια di Sp. P. Lampros," *Byzantinische Zeitschrift* 19 (1910): 580–81. For a list of the Argyropulus codices acquired by the Vatican Library, see A. Diller, "Greek Manuscripts Strayed from the Vatican Library," *Italia medioevale e umanistica* 26 (1983): 383–88, here 383, n. 1.

[12] For a good presentation of the life and importance of John Argyropulus, in addition to this note on the sale of his books, see D.J. Geanakoplos, *Constantinople and the West: Essays on the Late Byzantine (Palaeologan) and Italian Renaissances and the Byzantine*

few years before Lascaris came to Venice. We get an idea of their number when we see them grouped between numbers 34 and 58 on the B list below.

2. If the Argyropulus volumes were acquired in the second half of the 1480s, had Torriano previously acquired the 33 items preceding them on the B list? These items include three volumes (B15–17) Torriano used in his teaching before becoming Governor General of the Dominican Order in 1487. Could the other thirty, like these three items, have been in Torriano's possession in 1491 and been passed over by Lascaris?

If we look at the content of the thirty-three items in question, only one relates to entries on Lascaris' list of *desiderata*, speeches of Aeschines: Αἰσχίνου λόγοι δ′ (Mueller, "Mittheilungen," 10r 9). Item B11 (Marc. VIII, 4) contains speeches of Demosthenes and two speeches of Aeschines. This volume was obviously not available for sale and probably, since it offered only two desirable speeches of Aeschines, would not have been a prime candidate for copying.

In addition, if we subtract late grammars from the total of thirty-three (those of Torriano, Theodore Gaza, George Scholarius, and others which would have held little interest for Lorenzo), the twenty-six remaining items include only two authors not recorded as owned by Lorenzo. Of these Blemmydes, *Logica et physica* (B28) was already part of Lorenzo's library. Laurentianus 71.8 is a volume produced at his commission and surely known to Lascaris. Philostratus (B23) in Laur. 58.32 was in the Medici library in 1492 and probably before that. It was apparently known to Lascaris because he did not mention seeing Philostratus' works anywhere on his trip, nor did he include Philostratus among new authors he introduced to Florence. We might expect Lascaris to have taken note of Item 33, Nicetas David on Porphyry and Aristotle, a work Lorenzo de' Medici did not own. But Lascaris saw the same treatise at the home of Ermolao Barbaro and did make a note of it there. His Barbaro notes in Vat. 1412 follow those he made of Torriano's holdings, but we know nothing about Lascaris' process of visitation and note-taking, so this fact may not be significant.[13] It is quite possible then, and even likely, that the B list was begun by Torriano before 1487, that the first items on the list were the nucleus of his collection, and that he added to the list new acquisitions as they arrived. This would help to explain its apparent random presentation of authors and works. Small groupings of philosophica and grammatica would then point to the tastes of the owners from whom the volumes were purchased rather than an inability of Torriano to construct an orderly list.

---

and Roman Churches (Madison, WI, 1989), 91–113, esp. 111; also A.-M. Talbot, "Argyropoulos, John," in *Oxford Dictionary of Byzantium*, 3 vols. (New York, 1991), 1: 164–65.

[13] As an example of how unimportant the relative positioning of elements in Lascaris' notes can be, observe that the first items on his trip notes, preceding the Italian notations, are manuscripts purchased on the island of Corfu, a place he visited after the Italian sites.

3. Is there any reason to believe that the fifteen items (B59–73) that follow the Argyropulus volumes were not in Torriano's possession when Janus Lascaris visited him in 1491? Item B59, a psalter with glosses, would have drawn Lascaris' attention, as it did Richter and Gesner later. Item B62, Basil on Isaiah, does not appear to have been in Lorenzo's library. The anonymous commentary on Isaiah at B66 should also have caught Lascaris' eye. His list of *desiderata* includes exegeses of the New and Old Testaments: ἐξηγηταὶ τῆς θείας γραφῆς παλαιᾶς τε καὶ νέας (Mueller 10r19). Lorenzo owned Chrysostom's commentary on John, but not Matthew (B71). If, as Mioni believes, Marc. II, 3 (B72) comes from the same place and time as Marc. II, 2, then Augustine's treatise on the Trinity, as a *desideratum* (Αὐγουστίνου τὸ περὶ τριάδος ἑλληνικῶς [Mueller 9r15]), would certainly find its way onto Lascaris' list. The desire to find Byzantine histories, ἱστορικὰ νεωτέρων Ἑλλήνων . . . καὶ εἴ τι ἄλλον νέον ἱστορικὸν εὑρεθῇ (Mueller 9r 8–11) renders item B73, George Cedrenus et al., something he would have noted as well.

It is clear then that Gioachino Torriano had a small collection of Greek codices in the mid-1480s. Around that time he acquired a large number of manuscripts from John Argyropulus, added their descriptions to those of his earlier collection, and began a running list of new acquisitions. The items numbered B74 to B93 will later be shown to have been produced and/or purchased during the last years of Torriano's life.

II. Marcon's B List

By the time of his death in 1500 Gioachino Torriano had compiled a long list of manuscripts he had personally acquired for the library at Zanipolo, the inventory discussed at the end of Chapter I. This list consists of a short title and physical description of Greek texts (numbers 1–93) and Latin texts (numbers 94–233). The original list no longer exists, but when San Zanipolo transferred its holdings to the Marciana in 1789 a copy of the original was made by the Dominican D. M. Berardelli who had earlier composed the Zanipolo catalogue (see Introduction, n. 7). Berardelli made this copy of Torriano's list for Jacopo Morelli, who handled the transfer of the Zanipolo books to the Marciana. This copy is a recent discovery of and basis for an important publication by Susy Marcon of the Biblioteca Marciana.[1] Elpidio Mioni, in his catalogue of the additional manuscripts at the Marciana,[2] coupled each item in the Berardelli catalogue of 1770 with a volume presently in the Marciana along with its modern shelf number. Using these identifications, Marcon in turn recognized many of the items on the Torriano-Berardelli inventory. Because she called the inventory the B list, that designation is adopted here as well. What follows here is Marcon's transcription of Berardelli's copy of the Greek items from Torriano's original and her identifications of manuscripts presently at the Marciana. To these are added a few others at the Marciana which she did not identify, and several volumes which left Zanipolo before 1770, now located elsewhere:

Inventario fatto manu propria generalis ut hic apparet inferius.

Libri greci legati:

1. *Platonis dialogi in pergameno corio azuro coperti* (Marc. Gr. IV, 1). John Rhosus added supplementary folios to the start of this codex and Caesar Strategus to the end. Both, contrary to their usual practice, wrote in a two-column format to conform to the style of the old nucleus of the text.

---

[1] S. Marcon, "I libri del Generale Domenicano Gioachino Torriano nel convento Veneziano di San Zanipolo," *Miscellanea Marciana* 2–4 (1987–1989): 81–116.

[2] *Bibliothecae Divi Marci Venetiarum Codices Graeci Manuscripti*, ed. Mioni, 1: XXVII.

Aubrey Diller[3] has corrected past dating of this manuscript, recognizing in the main body of the text the hand of Ephraim the monk, of the tenth century. See below, Richter 27, Tomasini 19.

2. *Platonis dialogi sexdecim in papiro chorio nigro coperti*—There is no extant manuscript that matches this description. See Tomasini number 18 below for testimony that the now lost codex was still at San Zanipolo in the middle of the seventeenth century. See Richter 28.

3. *Platonis epistole cum tabulis sine chorio in papiro* = Marc. IV, 2 which contains Plato, *Definitiones* and *Epistolae* as well as the *De fato* of Theodore Gaza. The scribe is Francesco Vitale, who wrote several manuscripts for Torriano. The initial headpiece here is much like that in item 15 below. See Richter 100, Tomasini 55.

4. *Logica Aristotelis in papiro chorio rubeo coperta cum commento*. Commented examples of Aristotle's *Organon* and parts of the same are numerous. No extant manuscript of this description has as yet been tied to Zanipolo. It was still in Venice when Richter visited Zanipolo. See his number 55. The volume is not on Tomasini's list.

5. *Logica Aristotelis in pergameno sine commento seminigro coperta* (Marc. Gr. IV, 5). Porphyry's *Introduction* begins the text here, but the *Organon* which follows lacks commentary or any marginal scholia of note. See Tomasini 16. As was the case with several other commonly available items, Richter passed over this one in silence.

6. *Magnus Theodorus in philosophia in pergameno chorio zallo copertus*—A likely match for this item is today Parisinus gr. 2003, a parchment codex of the fourteenth century containing 120 philosophical and historical chapters of the Grand Logothete Theodore Metochites. In the front of the volume is a formal notice stating that it was a gift of "Clarissimi Viri Dominici Mauroceni Equitis et Senatoris Praestantiss. De omnium scientiarum studiis OPT. MERITI. . . ." Unfortunately the person or institution to which he gave the manuscript has been blacked out so as to be unreadable. The Morosini are a well-known Venetian family. Paolo Morosini, Venetian ambassador to the papal curia, persuaded Cardinal Bessarion to leave his wonderful library to the city of Venice.[4] He also, in 1503, presented to the Dominicans a Byzantine icon which was brought to Venice in 1349. Formerly installed in the *Scuola* of San Zanipolo, it was moved next door

---

[3] A. Diller, *Studies in Greek Manuscript Tradition* (Amsterdam, 1983), 254. Unless stated otherwise, identifications of scribal hands given here are based upon information given by Mioni in his catalogue or in E. Gamillscheg and D. Harlfinger, *Repertorium der griechischen Kopisten 800–1600, 1. Teil: HSS. aus Bibliotheken Grossbritanniens; 2. Teil: HSS. aus Bibliotheken Frankreichs; 3. Teil: HSS. aus Bibliotheken Roms mit dem Vatikan* (Vienna, 1981–1997).

[4] See Labowsky, *Bessarion's Library and the Biblioteca Marciana*, 24–25.

into the church in the nineteenth century and placed above the altar in the Chapel of Our Lady of Peace. Two other Morosini, a doge and a judge, are buried in that church. There is a Domenicus Maurocenus listed by Cosenza[5] to whom Matthew Collatius dedicated his *Opuscula* at Venice around 1486, a time that well suits Torriano's book-collecting activity. Paris. 2003 went to Paris in the collection of Jean Hurault de Boistaillé, French ambassador to Venice in the early 1560s. Hurault accumulated a large number of Greek manuscripts during a three-year stay in the city, many coming from religious communities including S. Antonio di Castello, S. Maria ab Orto, and Zanipolo. This codex seems to have belonged originally to Metochites himself.[6] On folio 7r the proem ends with an ornate series of monograms reading τοῦ μεγάλου θεολόγου μετοχίτου. See Richter 49.

7. *Thucidides in pergameno copertus chorio azuro.* This is Paris. suppl. gr. 255, the only one of the Zanipolo manuscripts carried off to Paris during the Napoleonic wars which was not returned to Venice. There is on folio 292v a note written by Theodore Metochites which creates an association with the previous item and indicates that Torriano acquired both manuscripts at the same time.[7] See Richter 74, Tomasini 73.

8. *Thucidides in pergameno chorio rubeo copertus* (Marc. Gr. VII, 5). Mioni implies that a note on folio 96 proclaims the end of Palla Strozzi marginalia in the codex. Actually the note refers to the end of Strozzi's work as text scribe. A new hand begins on fol. 96v. Strozzi's marginalia continue sporadically. Francesco de Lucha wrote on the front pastedown that he saw this manuscript.[8] See Richter 74, Tomasini 74.

9. *Suida in papiro chorio zalo copertus* (Marc. Gr. XI, 8). See Richter 85, Tomasini 2, where the material is said to be parchment, an error Tomasini often makes.

10. *Orationes Demostenis chorio zallo coperte* (Marc. Gr. VIII, 3). See Richter 67, Tomasini 49.

11. *Quedam orationes Demostenis et Eschinis in pergameno chorio zallo* (Marc. Gr. VIII, 4). See Richter 68, Tomasini 50.

---

[5] M. E. Cosenza, *Dictionary of Italian Humanists*, 6 vols. (Boston, 1962), 3: 2244.

[6] I. Ševčenko, *Etudes sur la polémique entre Théodore Métochite et Nicéphore Choumnos* (Brussels, 1962), 282 and n. 3; M. Arco Magrì, "Per una tradizione manoscritta dei Miscellanea di Teodoro Metochites," *Jahrbuch der Österreichischen Byzantinistik* 32/34 (1982): 49–69, here 56–57. For Jean Hurault see Jackson, "Greek Manuscripts."

[7] On the verso of the last front guard leaf of Paris. suppl. 255 is the note: *SS. Jean & paul de Venice, 88.* This is the number Berardelli records for the manuscript in his catalogue of 1770. For a detailed history and explanation of the entire transaction involving the codex, see J. Enoch Powell, *Classical Review* 50 (1936): 117–18.

[8] See M.L. Sosower, "Palla Strozzi's Greek Manuscripts," *Studi italiani di filologia classica* 3 (1986): 140–51, here 145.

12. *Polidorus, Eschilus, Esiodus, Theocritus, Dionisius Alicarnaseus in papiro chorio zallo copertus* (Marc. Gr. XI, 7). As Marcon notes, for Polidorus we should read *Pollux*, called Polydeuces at the end of his section (fol. 142r). *Dionysius Alexandreus* was misread as *Dionysius Alicarnaseus* for the fifth author. I believe that a long note on folio 247v is in the hand of Demetrius Chalcondyles. See Richter 87, Tomasini 36.
13. *Vocabolarium totum grecum in papiro chorio nigro copertum.* There is an Athanasius lexicon cited by Richter (his number 88 below) and Gesner (his number 2) which must be placed somewhere in this list. The lexicon left San Zanipolo and has not been identified. It seems the codex was somewhere marked clearly enough for Richter and Gesner to attribute authorship to Athanasius. Torriano either did not have or chose not to share this information. For Marcon's choice of Marc. X, 2 here see B77 below.
14. *Epistole Phalaridis et Bruti in papiro chorio zallo* (Marc. Gr. VIII, 11). Like item B3, much of this is the work of Francesco Vitale. See Richter 97, Tomasini 33.
15. *Vocabularium partim grecum partim latinum in papiro chorio viridi copertum* (Marc. Gr. X, 17). This is Torriano's own Greek grammar in his own hand. How many he made and distributed is not known. Marc. X, 18, another example, was previously owned by Pietro de Montagna (d. 1478) and left to S. Giovanni di Verdara of Padua, where it was when Torriano compiled his list. It came later to the Marciana. See Richter 86, Tomasini 23.
16. *Aliud vocabularium simile in papiro chorio rubeo copertum.* This duplicate of the previous item has not been identified.
17. *Aliud vocabularium in parvo volumine partim grecum partim latinum chorio rubeo.* This grammar, apparently the same as those of items 15 & 16, but in smaller format, has not been identified.
18. *Euripides quinque tragedie in papiro chorio rubeo* (Marc. Gr. IX, 11). See Richter 81, Tomasini 29.
19. *Alius Euripides antiquus in papiro cum asseribus* (Marc. Gr. IX, 12). See Richter 80.
20. *Plutarchi 22 paralelle in pergameno chorio rubeo* (Marc. Gr. IV, 55). See Richter 76, Tomasini 38.
21. *Commentarium super rethoricam Hermogenis in papiro chorio zallo.* This is Marc. XI, 2. The manuscript begins with Aesop and Planudes, but no author's name is mentioned in the text before Aphthonius and Hermogenes. At the back of the codex a Greek note says that it belonged to one ἰω. τοῦ κωνσταντή.[9] This is the medical doctor Joannes Constante who owned Marc. gr. 22, 57, and 403. See Richter 63, Tomasini 24.

---

[9] Constante also called this a grammar of Hermogenes. The next rear guard folio has the note "visto per me francesco de lucha". See footnote 8 above. Mioni misconstrues the name of the former owner.

22. *Orationes Libanii in papiro chorio rubeo* (Marc. Gr. VIII, 9). The last eight folios here are said to be by the late Byzantine grammarian Demetrius Triclinius and what precedes probably by a student of his.[10] See Richter 61, Tomasini 67.
23. *Icones Philostrati et eroica in papiro chorio rubeo* (Marc. Gr. XI, 15). Fifteen quires are missing from the front of this codex. Its fourteenth-century nucleus ends abruptly at the bottom of folio 135v and is followed by a two-folio fifteenth-century supplement. Callistratus on folio 1 lacks a title. Philostratus is thus the first author named. Several other authors are designated in the volume, but Torriano cited only the first and last works in the manuscript. See Richter 99, Gesner 13, Tomasini 66.
24. *Gramatica Moscopuli in papiro chorio zallo* (Marc. Gr. X, 3). This is a composite of several originally separate parts, but the volume was likely in the form we now have when Torriano described it. See Richter 96, Tomasini 75.
25. *Alia gramatica Moscopuli in pergameno cum expositione chorio rubeo* (Marc. Gr. X, 6). See Richter 94. An old label pasted to the front cover of this manuscript and another inside give the same title as Richter reports.
26. *Gramatica Theodori in papiro chorio nigro* (Marc. Gr. X, 11). This is another manuscript written by Francesco Vitale. See Richter 93, Tomasini 52.
27. *Declinationes verborum cum quibusdam aliis in papiro chorio zalo*. This may well be folios 55r and following in Marcianus X, 12. The two quires are not part of the original volume, though all was written by Francesco Vitale. These quires, marked α′ and β′, contain lists of verbs and the oblique cases each verb takes for its object—not declensions in the usual sense of the word. It is, of course, possible that another codex entirely is described here. Tomasini (his number 70) saw X, 12 as it is today.
28. *Niceforus, in logica et physica in pergameno in parvo volumine chorio rubeo*. Torriano's use of a praenomen here obscured from de Rachaneto that he was listing at A156 (see below) the same volume, Vaticanus Barberin. gr. 246. See A156 for more on the manuscript. The discovery that it was written for Torriano answers a question posed by Paul Canart who recognized in it a copy of Vaticanus gr. 315 made at Rome by Demetrius Damilas.[11] See Richter 48, Gesner I.516r.
29. *Moscopulus in papiro in rudimenta chorio nigro* (Marc. Gr. X, 5). See Richter 95.
30. *Gramatica Scolarii in papiro chorio rubeo* (Marc. Gr. X, 12). See item 27 above. The scribe is again Francesco Vitale. The Scholarius material and

---

[10] See Nigel Wilson, "Miscellanea Palaeographica," *Greek, Roman, and Byzantine Studies* 22 (1981): 395–404, here 397, and B. L. Fonkich, "Paleografičeskie zametki o grečeskikh rukopisakh bibliotek," *Vizantii Vremennik* 41 (1980): 210–20, cited by Wilson.

[11] P. Canart, "Demetrius Damilas, alias le 'Librarius Florentinus'," *Rivista di studi bizantini e neoelleniche* 24–26 (1977–1979): 281–347, here 315, 335.

some canons are written on quires marked α'–ζ'. The manuscript may not be as old as Mioni suggests. See Tomasini 70.

31. *Sinesii epistole in parvo volumine in pergameno chorio viridi.* Because parchment manuscripts of Synesius' letters are so numerous, this item may never be recognized. See Richter 11.

32. *Multi tractatus in papiro chorio quasi rubeo.* This item may be tentatively identified as Marc. V, 8. The title is vague enough to be applicable to another manuscript, but an old note on the first folio of Marc. V, 8 states that this volume was as a gift of Joachinus Torrianus. It should therefore be included on the B list. It should also be noted that folio 1 lacks the name of an author (referring only to the medicinal herb Hypericum), thus giving Torriano no help in identifying the first text. Mioni lists twenty-one different works between the covers. Wear on various folios indicates that the order of presentation of these items was not always as it is today. A former owner, the physician Constantine Meliteniotes (fol. 9v), wrote on a page of Oribasius/Dioscorides that this was Galen περὶ κρίσεων καὶ περὶ κρισίμων ἡμερῶν. Later inventories were influenced more by this note than by the esoteric herb in the first title. See Richter 17, Tomasini 28.

33. *David super Porphirio et predicamentis antiquus in papiro sine chorio.* There is only one old paper manuscript of Nicetas David on Porphyry's *Introduction* and Aristotle's *Categories* that will fit here. It is Parisinus gr. 1937, another codex Hurault de Boistaillé acquired in Venice early in the 1560s. His own note in the volume says he bought it from Andreas the Greek. Andreas Darmarius, along with his partner at the time, Nicolaus della Torre, provided the ambassador with most of the manuscripts that came to him from Venetian religious houses. This particular volume, dating to the fourteenth century, was in a bad state. Another note in the codex tells us that Hurault had the book repaired by Zacharias (Scordylis) and that he paid three times more for the repair than for the manuscript itself. Richter may have seen a reference to this volume and then referred to it only generally. See his number 55.

34. *Simplicius super predicamentis in papiro chorio viridi* (Marc. Gr. IV,14). This manuscript was written by John Argyropulus himself.[12] See Richter 57, Tomasini 8.

35. *Testus libri phisicorum in pergameno chorio nigro* (Marc. Gr. IV, 4). John Rhosus wrote this manuscript. It belonged once to John Argyropulus, as a note written by him at the bottom of folio 19v indicates. See Richter 34, Tomasini 25.

---

[12] See Mioni, Codices Graeci, ad loc.

36. *Simplicius super primo et secundo phisicorum in papiro chorio azuro* (Marc. Gr. IV, 15). Argyropulus wrote the text (Mioni, *Codices Graeci, ad loc.*) See Richter 36, Tomasini 9.
37. *Simplicius super tertio et quarto phisicorum chorio rubeo* (Marc. Gr. IV, 16). Written by John Argyropulus (Mioni, *Codices Graeci, ad loc.*) See Richter 37, Tomasini 10.
38. *Simplicius super quinto et sexto phisicorum chorio rubeo* (Marc. Gr. IV, 17). Written by John Argyropulus (Mioni, *Codices Graeci, ad loc.*) See Richter 37, Tomasini 11.
39. *Simplicius super septimo et octavo physicorum chorio rubeo* (Marc. Gr. IV, 18). Written by John Argyropulus (Mioni, *Codices Graeci, ad loc.*) See Richter 37, Tomasini 12.
40. *Philoponus super quarto phisicorum chorio rubeo* (Marc. Gr. IV, 20). Written by John Argyropulus (Mioni, *Codices Graeci, ad loc.*) See Lascaris 8, Richter 35, Tomasini 30.
41. *Alexander Aphrodiseus super libris metaurorum chorio azuro* (Marc. Gr. IV, 6; seen by Lascaris). Written by John Argyropulus (Mioni, *Codices Graeci, ad loc.*) See Lascaris 3, Richter 40, Tomasini 48.
42. *Simplicius super libris de anima chorio azuro* (Marc. Gr. IV, 19). Written by John Argyropulus (Mioni, *Codices Graeci, ad loc.*) See Lascaris 5, Richter 43, Tomasini 13.
43. *Parafrasis Themistii circa libros de anima chorio viridi* (Marc. Gr. IV, 13). Written by John Argyropulus (Mioni, *Codices Graeci, ad loc.*) See Lascaris 6, Tomasini 43.
44. *Parafrasis circa quinque primos libros ethycorum in papiro chorio rubeo* (Marc. Gr. IV, 21). On the pastedown there are titles from three different time periods. The first two name no author for the paraphrase. The third attributes it to Joseph the monk. See the next item. Marginalia here are likely by Argyropulus. This and the next volume certainly belonged to Argyropulus at one time. See Richter 53, Gesner I:397r-v, Tomasini 53.
45. *Parafrasis circa alios quinque in papiro chorio azuro* (Marc. Gr. IV, 22). A subscription after Book Six (fol. 31v) says that these volumes were written in the year 1366 at the expense of the former emperor, Joannes Cantacuzenus, now the monk Joasaph. Nicol has laid to rest the supposed authorship of

Joasaph for this paraphrase.[13] Nicol also lists other known examples of the paraphrase, among them several with the same subscription found here. Both volumes were formerly owned by John Argyropulus. See Richter 53, Tomasini 54, and Gesner 1: 397r–v.

46. *Plotinus in papiro chorio viridi.* This volume is now Parisinus gr. 1970. It once belonged to John Argyropulus and was written by him. It passed from Zanipolo to the de Mesmes family of Paris and with many of their manuscripts into the collection of Jean-Baptiste Colbert.[14] His vast collection entered the French royal library in 1732. See Richter 29.

47–48. *Rethorica Joseph ditis cum multis aliis tractatibus in papiro chorio rubeo.* Marcon glossed *ditis* as *Rhacendytes* and identified the volume as Marc. Gr. IV, 24. There are two problems with this suggestion. First, Marc. IV, 24 does not contain rhetorica. Second, there is nothing in that manuscript which would have led Torriano to attribute the work to the author whose name is incorrectly rendered in the B list description. It is better to associate Marc. IV, 24 with item 48: *De tota logica Aristotelis summatim cum multis aliis tractatibus in papiro chorio viridi.* As Marcon observes ("I libri," 105), when Janus Lascaris visited Torriano in 1491, he took note of item 48 and gave its incipit—σκοπὸς ἡμῖν ἐστιν θεοῦ συνάρσει, five words with which Marc. IV, 24 begins! See Lascaris 7, Richter 41, Tomasini 42. Where then are we to find a match for item 47? As it happens, the match is also at the Marciana, but it has not previously been recognized as a Zanipolo manuscript. Argyropulus, who owned both volumes discussed here, must have noticed that today's Marc. IV, 24 begins with a quire numbered six. He commissioned Demetrius Moschus to write a supplement of the missing material (Rhacendytes' rhetorica) and several other related works. These are today collected in Marc. VIII, 18, a volume that came to the Marciana from the monastery of S. Michele of Venice, but earlier belonged to Saints John and Paul. Unfortunately, Moschus' scribal work did not match the size of Marc. IV, 24. Rhacendytes' rhetorica in Marc. VIII, 18 (in the title of which the last two syllables of his name look like a word separate from what precedes and = *ditis*) are some 30 mm taller and 45 mm wider than

---

[13] D.M. Nicol, "A Paraphrase of the *Nicomachean Ethics* Attributed to the Emperor John VI Cantacuzene," *Byzantinoslavica* 29 (1968): 1–16. Nicol, without explanation, says Laurentianus 80.3, which he dates to the 14/15th century, is the oldest of the manuscripts with this subscription. Yet he dates our manuscript to the fourteenth century and Mioni makes a good case for its dating to the mid-fourteenth century. Nicol also says that Books Six through Ten of the Laurentianus date to the 15th century, while those in the Marcianus apparently were written by the same hand which precedes them. The rest of Nicol's exposition is quite informative.

[14] See D.F. Jackson, "Greek manuscripts of the de Mesmes family," *Scriptorium* 63 (2009) 89–121, here 101.

the paper in Marc. IV, 24. Moschus wrote the rhetorica on quires marked 1–5 and on folio 4v wrote: ἔχεις καὶ τοῦτο διὰ χειρὸς δημητρίου, a clear indication that it was intended as a supplement. He then wrote various other rhetorica on quires numbered 1–27. We can assume, then, since both B list items were bound at the time the list was compiled, that Torriano owned Marc. VIII, 18 in the same form as it is today. When the incomplete Rhacendytes philosophica, the Rhacendytes rhetorica, and the Greek rhetoricians were bound, content and relative size outweighed the importance of keeping varied works of the same author together. Moschus' texts became one manuscript which left the collection for a time, only to rejoin it later at the Marciana. This separation probably occurred quite early. Richter seems not to have seen it, nor, of course, did Tomasini.

49. *Sinesius de sopnis cum expositione chorio viridi in papiro* (Marc. Gr. XI, 9). Written by John Argyropulus (Mioni, *Codices Graeci, ad. loc.*) See Richter 52, Tomasini 63.

50. *Philoponus super duobus libris Nicomachi in gramatica chorio rubeo.* Richter (number 24 below) clears up an obvious error when he describes this as *Joannes Grammaticus in Nicomachi Arithmeticam.* We are therefore looking for a presentation of Philoponus' commentary with, probably, the text of Nicomachus Gerasenus. There exist several such codices old enough to be our manuscript. See Gesner 8.

51. *Proculus super primo libro Euclidis chorio quasi rubeo.* Proclus' commentary on book one of Euclid's *Elements* was a popular text late in the fifteenth and early in the sixteenth centuries. There are therefore several candidates for this Zanipolo item. Identification is both assisted and complicated by Richter (his number 23). When he refers to four commentaries of Proclus on Euclid, he seems to have mistaken a title which said that this was a commentary on Book One of *Elementa* in four books. Proclus did not comment on other works of Euclid. It is clear, however, that four works of Euclid, uncommented, followed. All five works were contained in the same volume, but Torriano mentioned only the first. Our best choice for identification is Parisinus gr. 2352, a composite of two parts, each produced separately by John Rhosus, a scribe who appears in other Torriano possessions. The first part carries a title proclaiming that this is a commentary of Proclus on book one of Euclid's *Elements* in four books. Richter's four works of Euclid follow: *Catoptrica, Phaenomena, Optica, Data.* Rhosus signed the Proclus section on folio 95 in August of 1487. The next part is written on paper very much like that which precedes and has a new sequence of quire numbers. Rhosus signed this section on folio 168 in February of 1488. Our manuscript came to Paris in the library of Jean Hurault de Boistaillé, as did several other Zanipolo codices. He acquired it in Venice early in the 1560s from Nicolaus della Torre, who, along with Andreas Darmarius, sold Hurault other Zanipolo manuscripts (Jackson, "Greek Manuscripts," 242).

52. *Theon et Pappus super Ptolomeo chorio rubeo.* These commentaries on the *Almagest* of Ptolemy are not rare, but most of the extant manuscripts old enough to qualify here have known histories which disqualify them from consideration. Two of lesser-known provenance are Toledo 98/14, reportedly written at Venice in 1488 by John Rhosus,[15] and Paris. gr. 2398 which formerly belonged to Hurault de Boistaillé. At one time believed to have been written by Caesar Strategus, but recently attributed to Demetrius Damilas by Paul Canart,[16] the Paris codex was produced for a private individual whose crest has been largely erased at text start. Two cherubs spray bright blue urine beside a crest, now largely scratched out, but formerly consisting of three vertical black stripes with gold stripes between. The connection with the French ambassador makes this the more attractive identification of the two.

53. *Dion de regno in papiro sine chorio.* Marcon took this to be Dio Cassius, but Richter (number 54 below), supported by Gesner (his number 5), describes the volume as *Dionis Chrisostomi in Philosophia Morali*. Since Torriano appears to be giving much less than full descriptions in this part of the B list, we should probably see *De regno* as the first of several orations which Richter and Gesner could then classify under the heading *Philosophia moralis*. They probably both got that designation from a library catalogue or the volume itself. No likely candidate can be offered here.

54. *Multi tractatus in grammatica in papiro chorio nigro sine tabulis.* We have already noted Zanipolo grammars that have disappeared (B 16–17 above). This is another.

55. *Multi tractatus diversorum in uno libro sine chorio.* For several reasons it seems best to identify this item as Parisinus gr. 2153. Janus Lascaris saw the third part of the manuscript (see his number 1 above) at the home of Torriano in 1491, and both Richter and Gesner saw other parts of it before it left Zanipolo. All of the works cited by Lascaris come from this portion of the B list, and this is the only suitable identification in the vicinity. Jean Hurault de Boistaillé purchased the volume at Venice early in the 1560s (Jackson, "Greek Manuscripts," 246). See Richter 15, 20, 42; Gesner 11.

56: *Quedam in rhetorica sine asseribus et sine chorio.* Marcon identified this volume as Marc. Gr. XI, 2, a codex discussed above at item 21. Richter (see his number 60 below) described item 56 in great detail. He, like Torriano, calls it *Quaedam in rhetorica* and goes on to say that it contains works of

---

[15] M. Vogel and V. Gardthausen, *Die Griechischen Schreiber des Mittelalters und der Renaissance* (Leipzig, 1909; repr. Hildesheim, 1966) 189. The year and scribe create an interesting connection with the previous item.

[16] Canart, "Demetrius Damilas," 334. Gamillscheg and Harlfinger disagree with Canart: see *Repertorium, 2. Teil*, pt. A, 66. The hand is very similar to that of Damilas, but different in some important details.

Aeschines, Apollonius (Dyscolus), and Phalaris. Richter was clearly looking at Marc. VIII, 2. The hand of Constantine Lascaris has recently been identified in a title (fol. 126r) and marginalia (fol. 199v) in this codex.[17] See Tomasini 4.

57. *Theophrasti multi tractatus in papiro chorio pellis leonis.* Richter (number 45 below) is of some assistance here: *Aristot: et Theophrasti parva animalia*. He seems to be referring to *Parva naturalia*, his description influenced by the presence of opuscula on animals. Aristotle and Theophrastus in their *opuscula* deal with some common topics, but it is unusual for the two authors and these topics to be found in the same volume. A few extant occurrences contain too many other works to fit the descriptions of Torriano and Richter. The known histories of others remove them from consideration. One attractive candidate remains. Paris. 1921 is a composite of at least two parts written by three scribes. The second part (folios 67 and following) begins with a *pinax* for a unique mix of Aristotle's *Parva naturalia*, short works on animals, and two *opuscula* of Theophrastus. Themistius on *De anima* also occurs, but appears to have escaped notice. The manuscript concludes with Philoponus on the astrolabe which Gesner (number 8) says he saw among the volumes at Zanipolo. It occurs nowhere else in the identified codices. Paris. 1921 has recently been confirmed as a Ridolfi manuscript.[18] Discovery of the hand of John Argyropulus in the margin of folio 52 increases the reliability of this identification and shows that at B57 we are still among the codices he once owned.[19]

58. *Simplicius super de celo et mundo azuro chopertus.* Both Janus Lascaris (number 4 above) in 1491 and Conrad Richter (number 39 below) in 1528 say that Torriano's volume held all four books of Simplicius' commentary. There appear to be only two extant manuscripts old enough and complete which fit this description: Ambrosianus C 253 inf. and Paris. 1910, written by John Rhosus at Rome. Dieter Harlfinger[20] has reported seeing John Argyropulus' hand in the margins of the latter. This news gives us both our best identification for the Zanipolo item and also how far down the B list Argyropulus' possessions extend. This is probably the last of the books on our list that belonged to Argyropulus. The Paris manuscript came to the BNF with the Colbert library. It had formerly belonged to Chandelier.

---

[17] T. Martinez Monzano, *Konstantinos Laskaris: Humanist, Philologe, Lehrer, Kopist* (Hamburg, 1994), 255, 284.

[18] See D. F. Jackson, "Unidentified Medicii-Regii Greek Codices," *Scriptorium* 54 (2000): 197–208, here 202.

[19] See Gamillscheg and Harlfinger, *Repertorium, 2. Teil,* pt. A, 93.

[20] Harlfinger, *Die Textgeschichte der Pseudo-aristotelischen Schrift* ΠΕΡΙ ΑΤΟΜΩΝ ΓΡΑΜΜΩΝ, 408. For Chandelier see D.F. Jackson, "Colbert Greek manuscript binding to 1675," *Codices Manuscripti* 66/67 (2008) 55–65, here 63.

59. *Psalterium magnum glosatum in pergameno in magno volumine zalo.* See Richter 2, Gesner 21 for more on this volume. It is yet to be identified.
60. *Unum aliud psalterium sine glosis in parvo volumine, rubeo* (Marc. gr. I, 1) The volume contains psalms, canticles, a menologion, triodium, and office of the Blessed Virgin. Lack of commentary and size clearly distinguish it from the previous item. Between the time of Torriano and Tomasini (number 75) no observers noted the existence of this codex.
61. *Eusebius Pamphilus de preparatione evangelica in papiro zalo.* Many possible identifications for this item exist.
62. *Expositio Basilii super Esaia propheta in pergameno chorio nigro.* = Parisinus gr. 495. This is another manuscript acquired by the French ambassador Jean Hurault de Boistaillé early in the 1560s. Almost all the San Zanipolo volumes that came to him were sold by either Andreas Darmarius or Nicolaus della Torre. The latter sold him this one. Although a parchment manuscript, this volume was not intended to be a part of the Torriano *pulcherrimi* which will be described later. It dates to the thirteenth century and its acquisition antedates Torriano's plans for that group. Size: 283 mm. x 210 mm. See Richter 5.
63. *Epistolae Pauli glosate chorio nigro in pergameno.* Not yet identified. This may well be the item listed as a volume of John Chrysostom at A142. Vielmi item 2 is Chrysostom on the Pauline epistles. See below.
64. *De processione Spiritus Sancti inter grecos et latinos in papiro nigro.* Marcon refers the reader to both Marc. II, 9 and II, 16. The description fits only the former. The other will appear at item B 69. The several parts of Marc. II, 9 were all done at the same place and close to the same time. A *pinax* at the start does not mention the first author, Nilus Cabasilas, probably the reason for Torriano not naming an author. But someone did offer on folio 1 *Sancti Hilarii sermones evangelici*, which seems to have resulted in a similar, now nearly illegible, paste-on to the front cover. See Tomasini 45.
65. *Iob glosatus in pergameno sine chorio cum asseribus.* Not yet identified. Richter at his number 4 saw this as an anonymous commentary on Job.
66. *Quedam expositio super Esaiam sine tabulis in pergameno.* Not yet identified.
67. *Biblia in pergameno usque ad Machabeos sine psalterio et prophetis in pergameno sine asseribus.* Not yet identified. See Richter 1, Gesner 20.
68. *Evangelistarium cum expositione in pergameno chorio rubeo.* Not identified. This is apparently what Richter refers to in his number 6, (passages from) the gospel of Matthew with an exposition.
69. *Alius de processione Spiritus Sancti chorio rubeo* = Marc. II, 16 (see item 64 above). This work of Manuel Calecas is bound in a leather cover with remnants of an old notice pasted to the front saying that it was a gift of Gioachino Torriano. See Tomasini 31.

70. *Exameron Joannis Chrisostomi ligatus rubeo in pergameno antiquus* is Marc. II, 4, twenty-four homilies of Chrysostom on Genesis dating to the eleventh century. See Richter 3, Tomasini 27.
71. *Expositio Ioannis Chrisostomi super Matheum chorio nigro* (Marc. Gr. II, 182). The folios in this codex presently numbered 1 and 2 contain a work of Gregory of Nyssa on the martyr Theodore. On folio 2v a contemporary note tells the reader to see the end of the manuscript for the rest of the work (on folio 354v). Between is the main content, thirty-six homilies of John Chrysostom on Matthew. See Richter 8, Tomasini 26.
72. *Duo libri ultimi contra Gentiles s. Thome in papiro rubeo* (Marc. Gr. II, 3). Marcon's identification is secure, but a complication arises in that Marc. II, 2, which now begins with two treatises formerly lacking titles, also contains portions of books 1–4 of *Contra gentiles*. In his catalogue Mioni reports that he has found the same watermark in both volumes, and reasonably suggests that both come from the same place at the same time. Both must also have belonged to Torriano. We should probably consider both volumes, in spite of a slight difference in size, as one when Torriano owned them. Richter offers no help. See Tomasini 58–59.
73. *Historia a principio mundi usque ad Osiam regem* (Marc. Gr. VII, 12). Alexander Turyn disagrees with Mioni's suggestion of a South Italian origin for this manuscript of George Cedrenus.[21] See Richter 75, Tomasini 17, Gesner 6.

Libri greci non ligati. The reason that these volumes were not bound is that they had only recently come into Torriano's possession. Three of them (items 75, 86, and 89) were written wholly or in part by scribes whose work appears earlier in the B list in bound volumes. The scribes reappear on the A list in unbound volumes written specifically for a project Torriano was pursuing late in his life. The rest were either written in the last years of the fifteenth century or acquired then by Torriano. Items 83 and 91 contradict the heading and were no doubt already bound when purchased.

74. *Homerus cum comento a litera N usque in finem in pergameno*. We cannot be sure whether Torriano's use of the capital letter here (if indeed it is his and not an introduction of a copyist) parallels modern usage in numbering books of the *Iliad*. In any case, no suitable manuscript of the *Odyssey* exists. The only extant *Iliad* manuscript on parchment beginning with the thirteenth book is Naples III-E-37. The text is accompanied by a paraphrase and is followed by *Batrachomyomachia*.
75. *Orationes Aristotelis in pergameno*. There is an obvious error in this description. We should read *Aristidis* for *Aristotelis*. The same error was made in

---

[21] A. Turyn, *Dated Greek Manuscripts of the 13th and 14th Centuries in the Libraries of Italy*, 2 vols. (Urbana, 1972), 1:47.

the Medici library inventory from c. 1495 in its description of Laur. 60.8.[22] The Zanipolo manuscript we seek is Marc. VIII, 7, a twelfth-century volume which lacked a beginning until Caesar Strategus supplemented the first six folios. Since much of Strategus' work was done in Florence, sometimes from Medici exemplars, there may be a causal connection between the wrongful attribution to Aristotle in the two codices. Aristotle's name here also led the A list compiler to believe that Marc. VIII, 7 had not yet been catalogued and he placed it at number 148 (see A list below). A note by Marcus Musurus on a front guard leaf states that the manuscript was a gift of Urbanus Bolzanius. The donation must have occurred long before the donor's death in 1524. See Richter 64, Tomasini 1.

76. *Esopus in greco et in latino a stampa in papiro*. Although there is an older Greco-Latin edition from Milan, this is probably the Venetian edition of Gabriel Bracius (1498). This gives us a good date for the acquisition of items around it.

77. *Eranus vocabulista in papiro*. The keys to understanding this description lie in one group of witnesses to pseudo-Zonaras' *Lexicon* and to the manuscript of Torriano itself. Mark Naoumides[23] cites six witnesses which employ the title Ἔρανος λέξεων in their titles. Of these only Copenhagen Add. 280, 4⁰ can be the one we seek. Below a braided ornamental headpiece on folio 1r someone other than the scribe wrote a simple Ἔρανος λέξεων. Above, next to the ex-libris of Thomas Bartholin (d. 1680), another hand wrote *Vocabularium*. Torriano evidently took Ἔρανος as a proper name and made him a vocabulary expert. The scribe Nicodemus signed the text in 1296 and added thirteen years later that his nephew had come to Patmos, giving us the likely place of his scribal activity. The volume passed from Bartholin to J.C. Kall and then to its present location. As with most lexica, Richter appears to have ignored this volume. Tomasini 77.

78. *Liber ethicorum Aristotelis in papiro*. This item description is too vague to warrant an attempt at identification.

79. *Apolonius et Orpheus argonauticon in papiro* = Marc. IX, 22. Mioni did not designate this a Zanipolo manuscript in his catalogue, but in his article[24] on the books of Marcus Musurus he said that folios 98 and following come from Zanipolo. Because one scribe is responsible for the whole volume and the same watermarks recur throughout, it is clear that we should consider

---

[22] Piccolomini, "Delle condizioni," *Archivio storico italiano* 20 (1874): 85, item 774.

[23] M. Naoumides, "The Shorter Version of Pseudo-Zonaras, *Lexicon*," in *Serta Turyniana*, ed. J.L. Heller (Urbana, 1974), 436–88. See the recent catalogue: B. Schartau, *Codices Graeci Haunienses* (Copenhagen, 1994) for a full description of the codex and a photograph of folio 1.

[24] E. Mioni, "La biblioteca greca di Marco Musuro," *Archivio Veneto* 93 (1971): 5–28, here 12.

Lycophron, who is found first in the codex, an original part of the manuscript. This section appears to be item A104 (below) on our lists. Apollonius of Rhodes is the only other author found in the codex today, but it seems that Orpheus was once part of the volume as well. What remains of the original came to the Marciana with the Bibliotheca Naniana. Separation from the Zanipolo collection must have occurred early. Richter mentions neither Apollonius nor Lycophron.

80. *Liber de anima Aristotelis in papiro.* Many possible candidates for this item exist. It was probably repeated by de Rachaneto as A102.
81. *Duo tractatus Proculi in astronomia.* The only extant manuscript containing two astronomical treatises of Proclus Diadochus seems to be Modena 24. This cannot be the volume sought, however, since Puntoni[25] has seen on its folios 61–62 several marginalia in the hand of George Valla. The Valla manuscripts at Modena belonged later to Alberto Pio of Carpi and eventually went to Modena. Both Torriano and Valla died in 1500.
82. *Duo tractatus in logica in papiro.* Gesner (number 8) says he saw at Zanipolo a commentary of John Philoponus on Aristotle's *Sophistici Elenchi.* This work does not appear by name on the Marcon lists. The only attested example of the text, in Parisinus gr. 1831, folio 127, begins with a note saying that the reason for a lack of a title is explained by the fact that some attribute the tract to Simplicius, some to Philoponus. Two preceding sections of Paris. 1831 were previously unconnected with the third part and are too late in date to have been Torriano possessions. The third part, however, is old enough and qualifies as *logica in papiro*. It is attractive for other reasons. The scribe is Emmanuel Zacharides, a co-worker with Arsenius Apostolis, whose earliest scribal activity dates to 1490.[26] The position of number 82 on the B list indicates a late purchase by Torriano, roughly contemporaneous with the parchment *pulcherrimi* (B 85, B 86, B 89) and the paper codex at B 84. Apostolis was an integral part of the *pulcherrimi* project discussed below which seems to have begun around 1494. What the second *logica* in B 82 might have been is not clear, but another tract by John Philoponus might be expected, since whoever had made the Philoponus identification of the second text by Gesner's time was likely led to it by the first tract in the manuscript. Paris. 1831 was part of the Fontainebleau collection and today has a binding of Henry II.
83. *Quedam pars Homeri iliados in papiro coperta pergameno.* Not identified.

---

[25] V. Puntoni, "Indice dei codici greci della Biblioteca Estense di Modena," *Studi italiani di filologia classica* 4 (1896): 379–536, here 396.

[26] See Gamillscheg and Harlfinger, *Repertorium 1. Teil*, pt. A, 76, and *2. Teil*, pt. A, 72. For Calliergis see the same volumes, 80 and 75.

84. *Commentum Alexandri Aphrodisei super topicam Aristotelis in papiro non completum.* Torriano borrowed such a work[27] from the Vatican Library in January of 1490 and returned it in May. Bertola believes it was Vat. gr. 270, a badly mutilated representative of the text. Torriano probably borrowed the Vatican manuscript to have it copied. The most likely identification for Torriano's copy is Paris. gr. 1832, part 2. This composite manuscript existed in the library of Cardinal Niccolò Ridolfi (d.1550) as three separate volumes.[28] Part 2 was a fairly late acquisition by Ridolfi. Anchor and Eagle watermarks in 1832, 2 are consistent with a date early in the 1490s, but whether or not it is a copy of the Vatican manuscript needs investigation. There is an intriguing circumstantial element in Paris. 1832 which may be a Torriano connection. When Cardinal Ridolfi died in 1550, his *philosophica* were in the process of rearrangement: plain texts, texts with commentary, and self-standing commentaries were being grouped separately. Parts 1 and 2 of Paris. 1832 were given the new numbers 54 and 46 *in capsa secunda*, previously being numbered 104 and 105. The latter numbers indicate both that they came late to Ridolfi (104 and 105 of 119 *philosophica*) and that they arrived at the same time or very close to the same time. Paris. 1832, 1 has in the front the inscription: *Fra Seraphino procurator della minerva*. Gioachino Torriano was buried at the Dominican community of S. Maria sopra Minerva at Rome.

85. *Commentum Ioannis gramatici super libris priorum Aristotelis.* Gesner (number 18) gives an incipit for this item: Ὁ σκοπὸς τῆς παρούσης πραγματείας διαπεφώνηται which, when taken with the Marcon description, identifies the commentary as one, lacking the name of an author, today found at folio 162 in Ambrosianus R 25 sup. at Milan. Maximus Tyrius (item A 143) precedes Philoponus. Duplicated excerpts from Proclus Diadochus on Plato's

---

[27] M. Bertòla, *I due primi registri di prestito della Biblioteca Apostolica Vaticana* (Vatican City, 1942), 81. For another possible linkage between Paris. 1832.2 and San Zanipolo see Ph. Hoffmann, "Autres données relatives à un mystérieux collaborateur d'Alde Manuce: l'Anonymus Harvardianus," *Mélanges de l'École Française de Rome Moyen-Age* 98 (1986): 673–708, here 681, where Hoffmann makes a tentative identification of the hand of Marcus Musurus, a scholar connected to the Zanipolo library in later chapters of this work, in margins of this part of the Paris manuscript.

[28] For Greek manuscripts acquired by Ridolfi before Zanipolo volumes began to be sold off, see D. F. Jackson, "An Old Book List Revisited: Greek Manuscripts of Janus Lascaris from the Library of Cardinal Niccolò Ridolfi," *Manuscripta* 43/44 (1999/2000): 77–133, and for manuscripts of Janus Lascaris acquired late in the 1520s, see idem, "A First Inventory of the Library of Cardinal Niccolò Ridolfi,"*Manuscripta* 45/46 (2001/2002): 49–77. Paris. 1832 appears on neither list and therefore came to Ridolfi during the period when Zanipolo manuscripts began to stray. For a comprehensive new study of the Cardinal's library, see Davide Muratore, La biblioteca del cardinale Niccolò Ridolfi, Edizioni dell' Orso, Alessandria 2009.

Cratylus which follow, lacking a title, appear to have always been associated with the *Prior analytics* commentary. The Ambrosian catalogue tells us that the codex belonged to Nicolaus Londa at Padua in 1552.[29] It is interesting that Torriano, who probably commissioned production of this parchment codex, knew who authored the Aristotle commentary but did not enter Philoponus' name into the manuscript. See Richter 30–31 for early association of the various parts noted here.

86. *Dionisius Alicarnaseus de arte* (Marc. Gr. VIII,10). This is a parchment codex written by Caesar Strategus in three parts, each distinguished by a change in the numbering of quires. The second part begins, oddly enough, with folio 161 in the middle of a single work by Aristides. The break in numbering therefore seems to have no significance. At a later time, however, folios 223 to the end were added to the volume. They are a later production of Strategus which is found below at A155. See Richter 69, Tomasini 60.

87. *Psalterium in papiro.* Not identified.

88. *Duodecim quinterni super duobus primis libris iliados Homeri in papiro.* See Marcon A 124 below and Gesner 1.

89. *Leges Platonis incomplete in pergameno* (Marc. Gr. XI,3). Plato, written by Francesco Vitale, ends abruptly on folio 397r. *Laws* is today preceded by *Etymologicum magnum* in the hand of Caesar Strategus (= A 149). Both belong to the group of *pulcherrimi* which will be discussed below. See Richter 91, Tomasini 3.

90. *Multi tractatus diversorum in diversis quinternis.* By a process of elimination this must be Marc. XI, 18. Torriano could surely have named several authors contained here, but he is decidedly terse in his descriptions in this section of the inventory. Richter (number 50) saw the manuscript. He names Theodorus (Gaza) who begins the volume, and gives 'Themistius' for Gemistus Pletho who is third, passing over in silence the Patriarch Gennadius who is not named in the codex either.[30] See Tomasini 68.

91. *Testus Aristotelis de celo et mundo; de meteoris et de anima in papiro ligatus sine asseribus.* Richter saw a volume beginning with *De caelo et mundo* and concluding with *De anima*, but he reports *De generatione et corruptione* between the two (his number 38 below). One of the two reporters is in error, or both works were present and each reporter selected a different one of the two to report. If the volume still exists, it can most likely be identified with Berlin Fol. 67 which lacks *Meteora*.

---

[29] *Catalogus codicum graecorum Bibliothecae Ambrosianae* digesserunt A. Martini et D. Bassi (Milan, 1906).

[30] Aubrey Diller, "The Autographs of Georgius Gemistus Pletho," *Scriptorium* 10 (1956): 27–41, here 41, says that Marc. XI, 18 in the Pletho excerpts is a copy of Marcianus gr. 379, probably written in Bessarion's circle or at Pletho's Mistra.

92. *Quadraginta tres quinterni in parvo volumine in pergameno non ligati.* The fact that this item appears at the end of the B list, that the material is parchment, and that the "volume" is unbound all point to these being works intended for inclusion among the *pulcherrimi* that were received by Torriano just before his death. The smallest *pulcherrimi* not mentioned specifically on the B list are Marc. X, 1 and XI, 14, the former today measuring 225 x 154 mm, the latter 224 x 155. In 1500 they were probably the same size and were stored together. Marc. X, 1 consists of 27 quires. Marc. XI, 14 begins with Eustathius Macrembolites' novel *Hysmine and Hysminias* with no generic connection to what follows. Caesar Strategus subscribed this section on folio 73v, demonstrating its independence from the rest. Folios 75 to the end consist of 16 full quires and a binion—very much what we seek. There are several other reasons to accept this conjunction of the two codices. Except for the *Histories* of Herodian in XI, 14, on quires numbered separately from what precedes and follows, the remaining contents of X, 1 and XI, 14 go together well thematically. Arsenius Apostolis wrote the first part of X, 1 and Caesar Strategus wrote all of XI, 14—two scribes intimately involved in the composition of the *pulcherrimi* at Florence. And finally, Marcus Musurus, whose connections with the *pulcherrimi* will be exposed at some length below, dedicated both Marc. X, 1 and XI, 14 to Alvise Bembo, writing πρῶτον and δεύτερον in them. He does not mean that these are the first and second volumes dedicated to Bembo, but, as he did with Appian of Marc. VII, 10, he is indicating his preference for order in binding. As we can see, the binder followed his instruction in neither case. Because Torriano gave no author names at B 92, de Rachaneto repeated these volumes on the A list. Dionysius and Hephestion of XI, 14 appear at A120, Apollonius, Hephestion, and Aelius Theon at A129 as unnamed grammatica, Herodian, now rightly extracted, at A144. See Richter 84 and 92, Tomasini 41 and 65.

93. *Epigrammata non ligata in papiro.* Not identified.

The number of unidentified manuscripts on the B list surpasses by far those on any other list. A dozen or so were seen by Richter and/or Gesner, indicating that these departed from Zanipolo after the 1530s, at the time during which most others left the collection, such as the many acquired by Jean Hurault de Boistaillé in the early 1560s. Others, however, were not seen by Richter. Since he often ignored grammars, lexica, and frequently-encountered religious texts, it is difficult to estimate with any confidence how many Torriano codices were not sent from Rome to Venice after his death in 1500. An unavoidable conclusion is, nonetheless, that at least a few remained in Rome.

III. Marcon's A List

The second part of Marcon's discovery is a transcription of an inventory composed soon after the death of Gioachino Torriano in 1500. She has designated it list A, a designation employed here as well. The A list was put together by a Dominican named Giovanni de Rachaneto, a member of the Zanipolo community whose incompetence, especially with Greek authors and texts, greatly complicates this study.

As Marcon has suggested, the community at San Zanipolo had some kind of library of its own apart from that which Torriano accumulated. A community library would have been both useful and necessary in pursuing its educational ends. Greek studies were evidently in the hands of Torriano before the house superior became governor general of the order in 1487 and began to spend much of his time in Rome. Instruction in Greek studies probably continued at Zanipolo after Torriano's elevation, although its quality could not have been very high, and a few Greek texts would have been useful in the house library. As will be suggested below, the return of Marcus Musurus to Venice at the end of the first decade of the sixteenth century probably solved the problem of Greek studies at San Zanipolo.

The first 88 items on the A list consist of a mix of Latin and Greek texts which may well include the community's library. Certainty about designating Greek texts in these first 88 items cannot be assumed, but four items should be mentioned here:

5. *Tute le opere de Galieno in bona carta a pena non ligato.* We should not suppose that this description is literally true, but the volume or volumes evidently contained a large collection of Galen's medical works distinct from, and probably the source for, Marc. V, 4 and V, 5 below (see the discussion and hypothesis offered in Appendix II). Because de Rachaneto included Marc. V, 4 and V, 5 among the *pulcherrimi*, it is likely that this Galen collection was a San Zanipolo possession separate from the library put together by Torriano. Its unbound state probably resulted from physical damage, not recent production. The entire manuscript has not survived, although parts may exist today.

6. *Eusebio de temporibus in bona carta scripto a pena senza tavole.* Marcon takes this to be a Latin translation and refers us to another at number A12. Since it follows closely on the Greek Galen of A5, there is a distinct possibility

that this item too was Greek. It is therefore necessary to keep an open mind about it.

57. *Eustachio greco in papiro non ligato.* Paul Canart, in his study of the hand of Demetrius Damilas, pointed out that Torriano borrowed a Vatican codex (*Eustracium in papiro super libros Ethicorum et Elenchorum*) of Eustratius in January 1494. It was returned by Damilas in November.[1] We can suppose that Torriano borrowed the volume to have it copied. This copy has not been identified, so whether the copying was carried out by Damilas or someone else is yet to be answered. See item A128 below, another unidentified but apparent copy of the first part of Vaticanus gr. 269, the volume borrowed from the Vatican.

88. *Uno libro in greco a pena sine titulo quinterni 13.* This appears to be Marc. V, 7, Galen *De compositione medicamentorum secundum locos.* Mioni notes that the present 23 quires are the result of recent dissolution of old quires and rebinding. If the older state of its 131 leaves was an arrangement of quinternions, the volume would have had 13 of these and an additional leaf. The text begins abruptly at book three without a title, thus explaining de Racheneto's *sine titulo.* See Richter 13.

The next group of books on the A list (items 91–106) consists of Greek texts, for the most part:

91. *Un libro greco sine titulo a pena in carta bambaxina non ligato quinterni numero 33.* This is probably Marc. V, 6, a Galen manuscript lacking a title before its abrupt beginning. The number of quires does not fit exactly, but the last quire signature, κη´ on folio 193r, is followed by 39 folios, some fourteenth-century originals, some fifteenth-century supplements, which may have looked like two more quires than the 31 now present. See Richter 19, Tomasini 78.

92. *Aristotele de mundo in greco non ligato.* Because of the summary nature of the descriptions in this part of the inventory we can picture this item as either a small number of folios containing only *De mundo* or a larger number containing several works, of which *De mundo* was first. Unidentified in either case.

93. *Alexandro Aphrodiseo non ligato.* Marcon has suggested Marc. IV, 10 for this item, but we shall see that that manuscript works better as number A126. Item 93 is Marc. IV, 7, Alexander on *Prior analytics 1.* See Richter 58, Tomasini 46.

94. *Psalterio greco a pena in bambaxina non ligato.* Not yet identified.

95. *Liber epitaphiorum in greco a pena non ligato.* This could be the last part of Marc. X, 15, two quires containing the *Oratio funebris* of Lysias, at this

---

[1] Canart, "Demetrius Damilas," 317. See also Bertòla, *Registri*, 84. *Elenchorum* here refers to Alexander of Aphrodisias on *Sophistici elenchi* which precedes the commentary on *Ethica Nicomachea* in the Vatican manuscript.

time separate from the unbound *grammatica* which now precede it. See item A106 below. It is more likely, however, that de Rachaneto is reading *Epistolae* as *Epitaphia* and is here looking at Marc. XI, 5. See Richter 10 below.

98. *Galieno de pulsibus in greco non ligato* = Parisinus gr. 2153, folios 47 to 169r. These folios contain various works of Galen on pulses which were once independent of surrounding material. Folios 170r–216v contain works of Avicenna and Galen which are ignored here. Richter (below, number 15) does account for them (see also Richter 42 and Gesner 11). Hurault de Boistaillé brought the codex to Paris.

99. *Verserio in greco non ligato*. This appears to be de Rachaneto's rendering of the almost illegible name *Actuarius* (τοῦ ὀκταρίου) on folio 290r of Paris. gr. 2153. (See preceding item and number one in Lascaris section above.) Item 99 probably includes everything in the Paris manuscript from folio 290 to the end.

100. *Orationes Demostenis in greco in bona carta non ligato*. Even though the majority of Demosthenes texts occur in paper codices, there are still far too many parchment *vetustiores* for a reasonable guess to be made about which was once at Zanipolo. We would expect Richter to have recorded this volume, had it been at Zanipolo in 1528.

101. *Plutarcho de institutione puerorum in greco non ligato*. If this is truly the whole content of the item described here, we have very few candidates for identification. The best choice is Laurentianus 80.25, a fifteenth-century codex containing only this opusculum and having no known history. It is not listed on the early Medici inventories. If this item is the same as Vielmi 18, he might well call the 17 folios of Laur. 80.25 a *libellus*.

102. *Aristoteles de anima in greco non ligato*. There are too many possible choices to risk a guess here. See item B80.

103. *La ethica de Aristotile ut supra*. The last two words in this description refer to item A21 which Marcon has identified as a Latin translation (= Marc. Lat. VI, 39). We should therefore consider A103 a Latin translation as well.

104. *Nitofano in greco a pena non ligato*. This is an inept attempt by de Rachaneto to identify Lycophron and his *Alexandra*. The poem is now properly attached to Apollonius of Rhodes, both written by the same scribe, in Marc. IX, 22. *Alexandra* has lost many folios, including its first quire, thus frustrating our ability to see exactly what de Rachaneto read. For the *Argonautica* portion of this codex see item B79 above.

105. *Uno libro in greco sine titulo in parvo folio quinterni numero 47*. This must be Marc. V, 9, today bound as two volumes. The first volume consists of 46 quires, the last of which contains the first part of book one of Galen *De simplicibus*. Book one concludes in the first quire of the second volume. It appears then that in de Rachaneto's time this manuscript of unwieldy size, 735 folios, had broken apart. Its first 44 quires were handled ineptly by him

at item A95 and the remaining 47 quires taken up here. It took some time for the two parts to be recognized as part of one whole. Richter reported them as separate entities (R14 and 16). The whole consists of an older medical nucleus and later additions by a student of John Argyropulus.[2] During the addition of passages this student also frequently altered quire numbering. See Tomasini 56.

106. *Luciano gramaticho in greco non ligato.* De Rachaneto appears to be referring here to Constantine Lascaris and his grammar = Marc. X, 15. Only the first 16 quires of the then-unbound manuscript would be involved here. For the last 2 quires see item A95.

After a few non-Greek items, we have item 114, *Una cassa de libri stampadi greci epitaphi in papiro*, then items A115 and A116, statements about payment for books made by Girolamo Contarini and de Rachaneto himself. The books came from Constantinople and Crete. Marcon has shown that de Rachaneto is first mentioned as part of the Zanipolo community in 1500, and his involvement with payment for and inventorying of library books probably started then, or soon after. Arrangements for the purchases mentioned here may well have been made by Torriano before 1500. Items 117–159, the end of Greek texts on the A list, form a very interesting group which does not come from the East. It bears the following heading: *Libri greci desligati in carta bona.*

117. *Teodoro Siculo* (Marc. Gr. VII, 7 and 8). Caesar Strategus wrote both volumes and signed the second at Florence. Mioni says that the exemplar of VII, 8 is Laurentianus 70.12,[3] a manuscript purchased at Constantinople by Janus Lascaris for Lorenzo de' Medici in 1491. F. Chamoux, on the other hand, says that the exemplar is Laur. 70.16,[4] a former possession of the monastery of San Marco in Florence. Size: 313 mm. x 212 mm. See Richter 77, Tomasini 62 and 34.

118. *Ariani partedia.* This is Marc. VII, 9, today containing both Arrian's *Anabasis Alexandri* and Polyaenus' *Strategemata*. Mioni described this as a paper manuscript without watermarks, before correcting to parchment in his *Ad-*

---

[2] See Mioni, *Codices Graeci*. The unidentified student of Argyropulus lists here his fellow students, as he did also in Oxford Barocci 87. See E. Legrand, *Bibliographie hellénique*, vol. 3 (Paris, 1903), 166a. These fellow students include Antonius and Manuel Pyropulus, Joannes Panaretus, Vranus Protomastor, Demetrius Angelus, Manuel Marulas, Agallon Moschus, and Andronicus Dioscurius Eparchus. Legrand gives a photo of the student's caricature drawing of Argyropulus as it appears in the Barocci codex, and part of the surrounding note. Geanakoplos reproduces the drawing on his cover and on page 97 of *Constantinople and the West.*

[3] See Mioni, *Codices Graeci*, 24.

[4] F. Chamoux and P. Bertrac, *Diodore de Sicile: Bibliothèque historique*, vol. 1 (Paris, 1993), LXXXVII.

denda. Both parts were written and signed by Caesar Strategus, the second part at Florence. It is unlikely that Polyaenus was associated with Arrian when de Rachaneto made his list. Size: 303 mm x 212 mm. See Richter 70, Tomasini 76 and item A 159 below.

119. *Polidorus.* This is probably best taken as the histories of Polybius in Marc. VII, 4. The scribe, Caesar Strategus, signed the manuscript at Florence. J.M. Moore[5] says VII, 4 is a copy of British Library Add. 11728 which was in the Badia at Florence during Strategus' lifetime. Size: 313 mm. x 212 mm. See Richter 72, Tomasini 14.

120. *Dionisio Alicarnaseo.* This is the third part of Marc. XI, 14, now preceded by Eustathius Macrembolites (not mentioned on our lists) and Herodianus (see item A144). Marcon suggested Marc. Gr. VII, 6 here, but that manuscript seems to better suit item A135. Strategus wrote and signed each of the three parts of XI, 14, but only the first part is distinguished as having been written in Florence. This is one of the few volumes in the group smaller than folio size: 224 mm x 155 mm. See item B92 above and R84, T65.

121. *Pindaron.* Marcon has suggested Marc. IX, 8 and IX, 9 here. The latter is a paper manuscript and would be out of place among unbound parchment items. It also seems to be a late addition to the Zanipolo collection. It was seen by Tomasini around 1650. Marc. IX, 8 works very nicely here. It was written by Strategus in two parts, each with his subscription. Like the previous item, this one is smaller than usual (237 mm x 160 mm). Jean Irigoin sees this Pindar as a copy of Parisinus gr. 2403,[6] formerly a possession of Cardinal Domenico Grimani (his number 120) and eventually sold to Jean Hurault by Nicolaus della Torre. See Jackson, "Greek Manuscripts," 224, and Richter 83, Tomasini 64.

122. *Aneochidi misteria* (Marc. Gr. VIII, 6), a collection of speeches by Andocides and other Attic orators. Nouhaud[7] sees Dinarchus here as deriving from Laurentianus 4.11, a manuscript Janus Lascaris purchased for the Medici on Mount Athos in 1492. The content and order of presentation of authors and orations in Marc. VIII, 6 make it very likely that it is wholly a copy of Laur. 4.11. Mioni originally attributed the writing of Marc. VIII, 6

---

[5] J. M. Moore, *The Manuscript Tradition of Polybius* (Cambridge, 1965), 12–13.

[6] J. Irigoin, *Histoire du texte de Pindare* (Paris, 1952), 378. Irigoin sees the dedication at the front of this volume as an *ex libris* of Marcus Musurus and the codex itself as one of several executed by Caesar Strategus for various prominent Venetians, a matter to be discussed below. He calls Marc. IX, 8 a faithful copy of Paris. gr. 2403, a volume Hurault de Boistaillé purchased from the Grimani collection at S. Antonio di Castello at Venice early in the 1560s.

[7] M. Nouhaud and L. Dors-Méary, *Dinarque: Discours* (Paris, 1990), XXIV, n. 68, where Reutzel is cited for derivation of Marc. VIII, 6 from Laur. 4.11.

to Caesar Strategus, but he later corrected to Aristobulus Apostolis.[8] Size: 310 mm x 217 mm. See Richter 65, Gesner 19, Tomasini 57

123. *Alexander Afrodiseus de sophistici* (Marc. Gr. IV, 8), a manuscript which contains two copies of the same work in two different hands. The first scribe is Aristobulus Apostolis. His text contains quire signatures similar to those in the Strategus manuscripts. The second text was attributed tentatively by Mioni to Demetrius Chalcondyles. My reaction is to disagree, but Dieter Harlfinger agrees with Mioni and his judgement carries great weight.[9] Although the size of the two parts is the same (295 mm x 205 mm), their handling of diagrams is different. The first incorporates diagrams into the text, while the second places them in the margins and creates a very different, less pleasing appearance. One of the two parts should be applied to item A128 below. One commentary probably comes from Vat. 269 (see A57 above). See Richter 58, Tomasini 47.

124. *Didimus super Homerum* = Marc. IX, 5. This Homer commentary has a note on its first guard leaf attributing the work to Didymus. Richter called it *Commentarii super Iliadem* (see his number 79). Marc. IX, 5 was written by Demetrius Damilas who was working in Rome in the mid-1490s for Torriano, as were Strategus and Apostolis at Florence. Size: 300 mm x 208 mm. See Tomasini 37. Gesner (see his number 1 below) saw an *Andronicus. Scholia in Homerum*. He was probably looking at the unidentified item B88 above. The name Andronicus is not found in Marc. IX, 5.

125. *Orationes Juliani*. An attractive identification for this item must, in the end, be abandoned. Vaticanus gr. 1448 was written by Demetrius Damilas, who played an important part in the formation of the group here being considered. But the Vatican codex contains, in addition to works of Julian, orations of Themistius, Libanius, and Isocrates as well. Gesner mentions only Julian (his number 9 below) for the Zanipolo codex, not surprising if the others were then available in print. But Richter (number 66) also describes the content as *Juliani Imperatoris Orationes*. It is unlikely that de Rachaneto, Gesner, and Richter would all overlook the added content. Marginalia by Jacob Questenberg also point to ownership by him and unlikely Zanipolo ownership. That the Zanipolo manuscript no longer exists is a strong possibility.

---

[8] Mioni, "La biblioteca greca di Marco Musuro," 16.

[9] See Harlfinger, *Repertorium, 2. Teil*, pt. A, 410. He credits only folios 159–295 to Chalcondyles. H. Buermann, "Handschriftliches zu den kleineren attischen Rednern," *Rheinisches Museum* 40 (1885): 387–97, here 390, has identified folios 44–47 of Marc. IV, 8 as formerly belonging to Vatican. Chis. R-VI-42. See also A.L. Di Lallo-Finuoli, "A proposito di alcuni codici Trincavelliani," *Rivista di studi bizantini e neoellenici* 24–26 (1977–1979): 349–76, here 354–55, where dating this manuscript to the last years of Marcus Musurus' life causes problems.

126. *Alexander Afrodiseus.* Marc. IV, 10 fits better here than Marcon's placement at A 93. This tall folio parchment codex (358 mm x 246 mm) was written by a scribe who does not appear elsewhere in the group, but in all other respects it fits nicely as a *pulcherrimus.* See Richter 46, Tomasini 15.
127. *Stephanus Bisantius.* This is the second half of Marc. XI, 12 (see also item A152). Both halves contain independent sets of quire numbers and were bound together because of relative length and size. *Ethnica* was written and signed by Caesar Strategus. Size: 310 mm x 225 mm. See Richter 90, Tomasini 40.
128. *Alexander Afrodiseus de elenchis.* See item A123 above.
129. *Gramaticha quedam sine titulo.* See item B92 above.
130. *Amoneo philosopho de quinque vocibus* (Marc. Gr. IV, 12). This is a manuscript written by Aristobulus Apostolis in the same style as the Strategus productions. Size: 315 mm x 225 mm. See Richter 56, Tomasini 32.
131. *Joanes storicus* (Marc. Gr. IV, 29). This Joannes Stobaeus manuscript was written by Demetrius Damilas. Paul Canart[10] recognizes this manuscript as a copy of Laurentianus 58.11, written in 1492 at Rome by John Rhosus. Marc. IV, 29 was then soon copied from it by Damilas and, in answer to Canart's question, for Gioachino Torriano. Size: 320 mm x 215 mm. See Richter 82, Tomasini 6.
132. *Alexander Aphrodiseus in topicam Aristotelis* (Marc. Gr. IV, 9). Aristobulus Apostolis is the scribe of this volume which measures 310 mm x 218 mm. See Richter 58, Tomasini 72.
133. *Sextus tanbegus* (Marc. Gr. IV, 26). Caesar Strategus wrote and signed the first 76 folios of this text of Sextus Empiricus. The rest is in the hand of Demetrius Damilas. Gioachino Torriano borrowed a manuscript of Sextus from the Vatican Library in January of 1494, and it was returned in November by Demetrius Damilas.[11] How and where Strategus was involved in the enterprise needs investigation. Size: 300 mm x 220 mm. See Gesner 16, Richter 32, Tomasini 21.
134. *Alexander Afrodiseus super parva naturalia.* Martin Richter saw this somewhat differently: *Alex: Aphrod: de sensu et sensato. Michaelis Ephesii in parva natural: Artis.* We are looking for a folio-size parchment codex with the latter content written by one of the usual scribes. Parisinus gr. 1882 has the right content and was written by Demetrius Damilas, thus rendering it a sure identification. Fryde[12] thought it a former Medici codex, but that is its twin, Monacensis gr. 151. The Paris manuscript was part of the Fontainebleau collection, bound during the reign of Henry II (1547–1559). Size: 290 mm x 180 mm. See Richter 44.

---

[10] Canart, "Demetrius Damilas," 305.
[11] Bertòla, *Registri,* 84.
[12] Fryde, *Greek Manuscripts,* 202

135. *Dionisio de antiquitate Romanorum* (Marc. Gr. VII, 6) . Caesar Strategus wrote and signed his work. Fromentin[13] says that it is a copy of Vaticanus Urbinas gr. 106 — a singular occurrence, if true. Fromentin's dating must be adjusted. Size: 315 mm x 219 mm. See Richter 73, Tomasini 22.
136. *Philoseno.* The author thus indicated is Syrianus Philoxenus. Both Richter (number 33) and Gesner (number 17) indicate that the text is Syrianus' commentary on Aristotle's *Metaphysics.* The only such codex which fits the time and style of this group is Montpellier, Ecole de Médecine 120, containing Syrianus' *Metaphysica, Dubia, De providentia.* It was acquired early in the 1560s by Jean Hurault de Boistaillé from Zanipolo, along with several more of its books, and entered the French royal collection in 1622 with most of his other manuscripts. The Rigault inventory number DXXXVII from that same year is still visible on folio 1r. The volume came to its present location with the library of the Bouhier family. Size: 296 mm x 207 mm.
137. *Philopato* = Marc. IX, 6. De Rachaneto was never successful in reading the ornate titles of Marcus Musurus, the scribe of this volume. He appears to have made no attempt at the names Hesiod and Cornutus (Pediasimus is untitled) and muddled the name of Palaephatus here. Richter saw this manuscript (his number 78 below), proving that it was in the collection in 1528. It belongs among Torriano's *pulcherrimi*, although an incomplete stemma on folio 1 indicates that it was produced for another patron who seems never to have taken possession of it. Size: 305 mm x 220 mm.
138. *Dionisius* [Periegetes]. This is Marc. XI, 13. Tsavari[14] says that it is a copy of Eton College 146. If this is true, the Eton manuscript would have to have been in Florence around 1495. Caesar Strategus wrote the Marcianus, and his subscription on folio 193v shows that the volume has always included Dionysius, Eustathius, and Simplicius, as it does today. Size: 310 mm x 210 mm. See Richter 47, Tomasini 7.
139. *Lisias* (Marc. Gr. VIII, 1). Aristobulus Apostolis wrote the text. Size: 311 mm x 220 mm. See Richter 62, Tomasini 44.
140. *Porphirio.* This item is today the second part of the three-part composite Marc. XI, 4, not previously identified as a Zanipolo manuscript, but recognized as the work of Aristobulus Apostolis by Mioni. Porphyry *De prosodia* begins on folio 106r with new quire signatures. An independent

---

[13] V. Fromentin, "Les manuscrits récents du livre I et l'épitomé des *Antiquités romaines* de Denys d'Halicarnasse," *Revue d'histoire des textes* 24 (1994): 100–2.

[14] I. O. Tsavari, *Histoire du texte de la Description de la terre de Denys le Periégète* (Joannina, 1990), description of Marc. XI, 7 on 202, Marc. XI, 13 on 203–4 and derivation of the latter on 281. For observations on and collations of the *Periegesis* in these two volumes, see N.A. Livadaras, "Ἡ Οἰκουμένης Περιήγησις ἐν τοῖς κώδιξι τῆς Μαρκιάνης Βιβλιοθήκης," *Thesaurismata* 3 (1964): 103–39. Discussion of the dedications in the front of Marc. XI, 13 should be ignored.

manuscript with a new set of quire marks begins on folio 156r (Dionysius Thrax, John Philoponus, and Ammonius) and is probably item A129 above, although the title there said to be lacking is now present. Both of these sections are preceded by Clement of Alexandria's *Paedagogus*, with its own quire signatures, a work not mentioned on our B list. Richter (number 89) and Gesner (number 3) saw it at San Zanipolo. Size: 310 mm x 220 mm.

141. *Eusebio de preparatione evangelica*. This is Parisinus gr. 466, written by Caesar Strategus. It came to the French royal collection in 1622 among the books of Jean Hurault de Boistaillé, who wrote in the front that he purchased it from the bookseller [Vincentio] Lucchino at Rome. Mras[15] says that the Paris manuscript is a direct copy of Laurentianus 6.9. That codex does not appear to have belonged to the Medici at the time. See Richter 7.

142. *Joanes Grisostomus*. Such meagre information renders identification of this item impossible. This may well be item B63 and Vielmi number 2 below.

143. *Maximo Tirio sophista in Thimeo Platonis*. How the last three words came to de Rachaneto is anyone's guess. Richter (see his number 30 below) saw the volume *in tertio pulpito: Maximi Tyrii Platonici opuscula*. Gesner (see 10 and 18 below) described it as *philosophicae quaestiones sive sermones vel capita 41*. This information allows us to identify the Zanipolo text as the first part of the composite Ambrosianus R 25 sup. It is followed at folio 162 by [Philoponus'] commentary on the *Prior analytics* of Aristotle (= B85 above). No scribal hands have been reported. The size of the codex is small (222 mm x 158 mm.), but it is, like the other *pulcherrimi*, parchment. As was noted above at B85, Nicolaus Londa of Padua acquired the manuscript in 1552.

144. *Herodianus*. This item is found in another composite codex, Marc. XI, 14 (see item A120 above). Herodian, *De Caesaribus*, begins on folio 75r on 13 quinternions numbered independently. Caesar Strategus wrote and signed this part of the volume, but did not include the place of writing, unlike the Eustathius Macrembolites (Florence) which precedes. Cataldi Palau says that the text of the novel comes from Paris. gr. 2915, a codex Janus Lascaris seems to have acquired in the East.[16] See item B92 above and Richter 84, Tomasini 65 below. Size: 224 mm x 155 mm.

145. *Gramatica quinterni 4*. Not identified.

---

[15] K. Mras, *Eusebius Werke*, 8. Bd.: *Die Praeparatio evangelica, Erster Teil* (Berlin, 1954), XLI, as cited by M. Sicherl, "Musuros-Handschriften," in *Serta Turyniana*, 564–608, here 597.

[16] A. Cataldi Palau, "La tradition manuscrite d'Eustathe Makrembolitès," *Revue d'histoire des textes* 10 (1980): 75–113 and Jackson, "A New Look at an Old Book List," 96–97. At the times of writing our articles we both accepted the then current belief that Marc. XI, 14 had been a Musurus manuscript. Information to the contrary presented below creates no impediment to believing Cataldi Palau's manuscript relationships (93–99), although dating has to be altered.

146. *Arpocrationis de dictionibus.* This is today the second half of Geneva Bodmer 43 (Omont 158). Caesar Strategus wrote the second part of this parchment codex and signed it at Florence. Harpocration is preceded by Procopius *De aedificiis Justiniani* in the hand of Aristobulus Apostolis. This work is not found on either of Marcon's lists. It is certain, however, that both parts come from Zanipolo. This is assured by the scribes, the material, the size, and the fact that Richter in 1528 (see his number 98 below) saw the volume in this state. Omont[17] reports that the first folio now bears the arms of Charles Cardinal of Lorraine, an office he held from 1555 to 1574. The cardinal had much other decoration added to the manuscript, which also bears the inventory number 229 of Alexander Petau. Size: 208 mm x 148 mm.

147. *Unus liber anticus sine principio et fine.* This is probably Marc. XI, 1, a thirteenth-century parchment palimpsest lacking its beginning and end. The first five works in this miscellany lack titles, a lack which prevented a more helpful description. Format is much smaller than that of other codices in this group. Size: 140 mm x 115 mm.

148. *Alter liber ut supra* = Marc. VIII, 7. This manuscript appears on our lists also as B75 (q.v.). The Aristides text was there attributed to Aristotle, causing a confusion which resulted in the repetition here. Size: 324 mm x 236 mm.

149. *Quatuor quinterni sine titulo quorum principium est: Alpha in magno folio.* There is here an apparent *lapsus calami* by either de Rachaneto or Berardelli. The volume is part one of Marc. XI, 3 (see B89 above). This part of the composite codex was written by Caesar Strategus on 34, not 4, quires. It is the *Etymologicum magnum* beginning [Ἄ]λφα τὸ στοιχεῖον. This half of the volume has been cut down substantially from its former state so as to make it conform to the size of the following section written by Francesco Vitale. Even so, it is 388 mm x 265 mm in size. See Richter 91, Tomasini 3.

150. *Liber antiquus ut supra sine titulo quinterni 3.* Not identified, but probably one of the mathematical texts recorded by Richter at numbers 25 and 26.

151. *Opera Galieni in bona carta quinterni 45.* Marcon discounts the possibility that this is Marc. V, 4 and 5. Both were written by Caesar Strategus. Marc. V, 4 consists of 31 quires to which Strategus signed his name. Marc. V, 5 consists of 46 quires numbered α'– λβ' and α'– ιδ'. Thus the end of V, 5, in its unbound state, was taken by de Rachaneto with what is now Marc. V, 4 to total 45 quires. The first 32 quires of Marc. V, 5 constitute item A153 below. For both manuscripts see the discussion in Appendix II. Marc. V, 4 now measures 388 mm x 275 mm and V, 5 is 390 mm x 270 mm. See Richter 20.

152. *Opera sine titulo in magno folio quinterni 34.* This is Marc. XI, 12, another composite codex. The first 15 quinternions, containing Cassianus Bassus, were written by Marcus Musurus. De Rachaneto consistently had trouble

---

[17] H. Omont, "Catalogue des manuscrits grecs des bibliothèques de Suisse," *Centralblatt für Bibliothekswesen* 3 (1886): 385–452, here 438.

reading Musurus' titles and evidently could not make sense of his *pinax* here. Stephanus Byzantius, lacking a title, occupies the last 19 quires, written by Caesar Strategus. Size: 310 mm x 225 mm. See Richter 90, Tomasini 40.

153. *Aforismi in magno folio quinterni* 32. See item A151 above.
154. *Liber de vitiis urinarum quinterniones* 27. Not identified
155. *Alcibiades*. Marc. VIII, 10 is a composite manuscript mentioned earlier at number 86 of the B list. The whole volume was written by Caesar Strategus, but folio 223r begins a new series of quire numbers for texts of [Sopater and Cyrus]. Having only an initial paragraph heading (Μετὰ τὰ κατὰ Κύζικον Ἀλκιβιάδης αἰτήσας φρουρὰν. . .) and the paragraph beginning on [Α]ὐθάδης ἐστὶν Ἀλκιβιάδη. . . . de Rachaneto entered the one-word title for item A155. See Richter 69, Tomasini 60. Size: 298 mm x 212 mm.
156. *Blemidas*. Richter (his number 48) tells us that this is *Blemidis Epitome Philosophiae*. Gesner (number 12) says he saw the volume, that it is folio size and about one and one-half fingers thick. A finger usually amounts to 75–80 folios. This should be a folio-size parchment codex of about 120 folios, preferably written by one of our *pulcherrimi* scribes. This volume of logic and physics by Nicephorus Blemmydes is today Vaticanus Barberinianus gr. 246, written by Demetrius Damilas. The scribe borrowed such a text (Vatic. gr. 315) from the Vatican Library in the name of the *padre generale di santo Dominico* in March of 1494 and returned it in November,[18] thereby presenting a dependable date for the writing of the Barberini codex. See B28 above, Richter 48, Gesner 12. Size: 305 mm x 215 mm.
157. *Liber sine titulo quinterni* 28. This is Marc. IX, 10 which contains seven tragedies of Euripides and a final epigram by Marcus Musurus, the scribe of the manuscript. As usual, de Rachaneto had no luck in reading Musurus' titles, in this case not even trying to transliterate them. There is no doubt, however, that the parchment volume belongs among Torriano's *pulcherrimi*. In Musurus' concluding epigram he says he wrote the text at the behest of Torriano. The manuscript consists of 27 full quires and a single final folio which was probably once followed by others. The final folio is paper containing a few words and several numbers written by Musurus, perhaps as an exercise. The watermark on this sheet is close to Briquet 4895 which dates to A.D. 1498. Size: 310 mm x 228 mm. See Richter 80, Tomasini 35.
158. *Quinterniones scripti in magno folio in bona carta* 30. Marc. VII, 10 is an untitled manuscript of the works of Appian written by Caesar Strategus. Mervin Dilts says that the text comes from two exemplars, Breslau Rehdiger 14 (in Italy as early as 1470) and Laurentianus 70.33.[19] The latter

---

[18] See Bertòla, *Registri*, 60–61 and Canart, "Demetrius Damilas," 315, 335.

[19] M. R. Dilts, "The Manuscripts of Appian's *Historia Romana*," *Revue d'histoire des textes* 1 (1971): 49–71, here 57.

belonged to the public library of San Marco at Florence and became part of the Medici collection in the sixteenth century. The presentation of books in Marc. VII, 10 is disordered. Books 3 through 5 of *Romaika* come first, ending with a blank folio 100 (end of quire 10) upon which Marcus Musurus wrote δεύτερον. Folio 101 is blank and discolored as though once used as a guard leaf. Musurus wrote upon it πρῶτον. Binders of the book appear to have paid no attention to his directive.The text of *Keltika* etc. begins on folio 102 with a new set of quire signatures running through number 20. The volume ends with books 1 and 2 of *Romaika*. Size: 302 mm x 211 mm. See Richter 71, Tomasini 39.

159. *Alii quinterni non sic magni in bona carta quamplures.* These must be the last of the *pulcherrimi* delivered to Torriano before his death. Members of the group not identifiable on the B or A list include: part 2 of Marc. VII, 9, Marc. IX, 6, Marc. XI, 4 and part 1 of Marc. XI, 12. See Richter 70, 78, 89, and 90, Gesner 1:188v and I.562v, 1:177r and 1: 529v, Tomasini 76, 5, and 40.

160. *Carte de vitello per uno lectionario.* There is no indication that this project was ever carried out.

IV. Gioachino Torriano's Grand Plan

The group of largely folio-size parchment codices with which the last chapter ended, taken together with several items from the end of the B list (75, 85, 86, 89 and 92) in Chapter II, are clear evidence that Gioachino Torriano had a larger plan in mind than simply collecting texts of ancient Greek and Byzantine authors. Had this been his sole purpose, smaller and less expensive paper codices would have served, as they had in the earlier stages of his collecting. Instead he commissioned scribes like Caesar Strategus, Aristobulus Apostolis, Demetrius Damilas, and Marcus Musurus to compose for him books of imposing size and beauty at great expense to himself and/or the Dominican Order. Some few, those included on the B list, were delivered to him and inventoried before his death in 1500. Other manuscripts, in greater numbers, arrived in Venice soon after his death and were inventoried by Giovanni de Rachaneto as a group of unbound parchment volumes. Others, found on neither of these inventories, appear to have arrived even later, payment for them perhaps having been made before Torriano's death and therefore properly turned over to the community of San Zanipolo.

These facts prompt the inevitable question: What was Torriano's purpose in creating such wonderful volumes? They could hardly be justified as objects intended *ad usum Torriani* as a private individual. Nor would they be particularly useful as study aids for boys instructed at Zanipolo. Torriano, formerly teacher of Greek in the school, was himself now living most of his days in Rome, and the school at Zanipolo seems to have offered at this time no better teacher of Greek than the clearly inadequate author of the A list. To answer the question we must go back to Venetian acquisition of an earlier library.

The beginnings of Venetian interest in a municipal library which would rank it among the great cultural centers of the Renaissance originate with the city's campaign to gain possession of the large Greek library of Cardinal Bessarion, a library that the cardinal had assiduously collected and produced, not altogether from a desire to accommodate his own scholarly interests and those of his friends. With the fall of Constantinople in 1453 he feared the loss of his ancestral cultural and literary legacy. In 1454/55 he wrote to Michael Apostolis and Theophanes of Athens about his desire to construct a library of all Greek literature.[1] He enclosed with these letters a list of *desiderata* which has since been lost. Both of his correspondents seem to have cooperated in buying texts, and Apostolis also served as one of Bessarion's chief scribes in producing new manuscripts. But assembling old witnesses and copies of old witnesses was not Bessarion's prime concern. He used his acquisitions to serve as the basis for the production of imposing texts of numerous authors which he called *pulcherrimi*, beautiful parchment codices, usually folio-size.[2] My own count of these *pulcherrimi* presently in the old collection of the Marciana comes to some eighty Greek codices. Of these forty-four measure 300 mm or more in height and thirty-one others between 250 and 299 mm, all well within the limits of folio-size volumes. Scribes most often employed in writing the *pulcherrimi*, each executing eighteen volumes, were George Trivizias and John Rhosus, both known for their attractive and legible calligraphic script. Others in the group, also writing in a clear and attractive style, are George Tzangaropulus (five volumes), John Plusiadenus (seven volumes), Andronicus Callistus (five volumes), and Michael Apostolis, who wrote ten volumes.

There appears to have been no attempt to improve the quality of texts involved in Torriano's production of new manuscripts, but the parallel between his desire to create a large number of beautiful codices and that of Cardinal Bessarion's earlier project are too clear to be ignored. The cardinal had stipulated that his manuscripts were to be available to the general public for reading and research,[3] a stipulation not fulfilled until long after even Torriano's lifetime. Because both scholars and non-scholarly readers were to be encouraged to use his library, Bessarion made his books both physically attractive and durable. The eighty parchment manuscripts mentioned above thus offer excellent texts for study, and artistic ornamentation for a more general esthetic appeal, resulting in his apt name for them, *pulcherrimi*. Torriano too had his scribes lay out their texts in such a way as to allow for later insertion of artistic headpieces, titles, and initials, a consummation never realized. Beautiful bindings, no doubt also part of his plan, had not been provided at the time the A list was compiled by de Rachaneto. Torriano assembled scribes whose hands, like those of Bessarion's scribes, were large, well-rounded, and attractive. Most frequently represented is Caesar Strategus, whose hand so resembles that of John Rhosus that the two have often been mistaken for each other. Frequently found, in addition, are Demetrius Damilas, Strategus' Roman counterpart, and Aristobulus Apostolis, son of Bessarion's Michael, his hand similar in style to his father's. Marcus

---

[1] Virtually all of the information recorded here which has to do with Cardinal Bessarion is taken from Labowsky, *Bessarion's Library*. For Bessarion's letters to Apostolis and Theophanes see 13, 14. A more detailed study of some aspects of the acquisition and maintenance of Bessarion's manuscripts is contained in Zorzi, "Bessarione e i codici greci."

[2] Labowsky, *Bessarion's Library*, 14, 15

[3] See Labowsky, *Bessarion's Library*, 153–56, *Instrumentum donationis librorum*.

Musurus, whose normal script is attractive and readable, was also involved in writing a few of the manuscripts. His ornate titles posed severe problems for de Rachaneto. But we should not be misled into thinking that Torriano's plan was to create a collection to rival Bessarion's. As will be shown in Appendix I below, his *pulcherrimi* were to serve as a complement to those of Bessarion, because Torriano had a much more ambitious plan in mind.

In order to convince Cardinal Bessarion to revoke earlier designated legatees and confer his book collection on the city of Venice, the Senate had promised to construct a library in the neighborhood of the cathedral of San Marco and to name it after the city's patron saint. Shipment of books began in 1467 and was completed soon after the cardinal's death in 1472. The legacy was "temporarily" housed in a room in the Palace of the Doges between San Marco and the lagoon. In a short time this room was needed for increasing municipal services, so the manuscripts were crated up and placed behind a makeshift partition[4] — a situation which severely hampered consultation of texts, something not encouraged by the Senate in any case.

A few senators, who had hoped that the previously planned library would come into being before the books suffered harm from disuse and humidity, periodically raised the question of when the solemn promises made to Cardinal Bessarion would be fulfilled. Little came of their efforts. It was probably these senators, however, who encouraged Gioachino Torriano to make a surprising appeal to the Venetian Senate.[5]

In 1494 Torriano made a formal proposal to the Venetian Senate that, if they would permit Bessarion's collection to be joined with the collection he had acquired and would continue to accumulate, the Dominicans would construct a new and suitable library at San Zanipolo and name it after Saint Mark. Although this location was out of sight of San Marco, the Senate accepted the proposal and went so far as to transfer to Zanipolo the expensive desks which they had had made for their own proposed, but still non-existent, library. These appear to be the *pulpiti* referred to by Richter below as locations for Zanipolo manuscripts in his time. The Senate laid heavy by-laws on the handling of the "*libri Nicaeni*" which would still belong to the city of Venice and remain under the supervision of the Senate. But before the new library was constructed and Bessarion's books relocated, Torriano died. The community at Zanipolo subsequently allowed Torriano's undertaking to stagnate and perish. Thus, were it not for inertia on the part of survivors on either side of the agreement, the Biblioteca Marciana could have opened much sooner than it did and in quite a different place. Deprived of the intended union with the library of Bessarion, the Governor General's

---

[4] Labowsky, *Bessarion's Library*, 57–59; Zorzi, "Bessarione e i codici greci," 113, 119; Lowry, "Two Great Venetian Libraries in the Age of Aldus Manutius," 133–66.

[5] Labowsky, *Bessarion's Library*, 60–61.

pulcherrimi and other manuscripts meanwhile lay unused, many unbound, undecorated, and largely badly catalogued for several years.

The proposed connection between Torriano's library and the collection of Cardinal Bessarion clarifies considerably the relationship between the two sets of *pulcherrimi*. In addition, the time of the proposal to the Venetian Senate and its acceptance are determinants in dating the copying of Torriano's *pulcherrimi*, which he seems to have begun only after union of the two collections seemed about to become a reality. Reliable dating of these manuscripts has previously been impossible because of the long period of scribal activity enjoyed by their copyists, because ownership of the manuscripts themselves has been confused (see Chapter V below), and because parchment does not offer dating information that watermarks on paper provide.

A document dated 2 June 1494 in which several *Consiliarii* and *Sapientes* refer to the already completed agreement with Torriano is helpful in establishing a more definite date for the writing of the *pulcherrimi*.[6] It is also significant that one of two Vatican manuscripts borrowed by Torriano in January of 1494 and returned in November by Demetrius Damilas served as an exemplar for a parchment codex (Marc. IV, 26 = A133), the other as exemplar for a paper manuscript (= A57).[7] The as-yet unidentified *Eustachio* was probably written first, before the agreement between Torriano and the Senate was reached, Sextus Empiricus after agreement was reached, or perhaps a little earlier, when prospects for agreement were good. We can, at any rate, see the inception of the folio-size, parchment manuscript project as dating from the first half of the year 1494. Additional proof of this timeline is offered by a record stating that *Demetrio Cretense, scritore in greco* borrowed a Blemmydes philosophical manuscript from the Vatican (Vat. gr. 315) in the name of *lo reverendissimo padre generale di santo Dominico* on 17 May 1494 and returned it on 15 November.[8] The resulting copy of this loan is item A156 above. Not only can the origins of Torriano's project be established through Vatican loans, but the *pulcherrimi* can also be used to clarify Vatican loan records. A manuscript of Didymus' lexicon to Homer's *Iliad* (Vat. gr. 32) was loaned by the Vatican Library to Marcus de Salerno on 10 December 1492. The volume was returned on 9 March with no year given. The same day the volume was borrowed by *Demetrio Cretense, scritore in greco*.[9] It appears that Damilas recalled the book for his own use and removed it from the library immediately upon its return, so as to be able to copy from it item A124 above. Loans lasting

---

[6] Labowsky, *Bessarion's Library*, Document VIII, 128–29. Berardelli in his Zanipolo catalogue of 1770 (165–67) records the agreement between Torriano and the Venetian Senate, giving the date as 11 June 1494.

[7] Bertòla, *Registri*, 84.

[8] Bertòla, *Registri*, 60–61.

[9] Bertòla, *Registri*, 102.

more than a year were not unusual at the Vatican in the 1490s, so it appears that 9 March was in the year 1494, not 1493.

Just as Damilas was beginning one half of the *pulcherrimi* project at Rome during the first half of 1494, so too Caesar Strategus and Aristobulus Apostolis were beginning the other half at Florence. Damilas and Strategus may even have met to compare notes and methods at this time, resulting in item A133, the Sextus Empiricus in which they both had a hand. Their project to create beautiful, large manuscripts modeled largely on those earlier produced for Cardinal Bessarion would, when the new Biblioteca Marciana was opened, indicate how much the Dominican community was contributing to the venture being celebrated.

V. The *Pulcherrimi* and Marcus Musurus

Having established that the folio-size parchment codices of Saints John and Paul at Venice were created as a commisssion of Gioachino Torriano between the years 1494 and 1500, we must now turn to the work of two respected scholars who independently came to the conclusion that these volumes had once belonged to Marcus Musurus. In order to give their conclusion the attention it deserves (while having already demonstrated that these manuscripts always belonged to San Zanipolo), it will be well briefly to summarize the life and accomplishments of the man whose involvement with the *pulcherrimi* will be shown to have been scribal and, for a time, curatorial.

Marcus Musurus was born on Crete and in 1486, as a young man, went to Florence to be educated in the school and learned circle around Lorenzo de' Medici. Among his fellow students were Aristobulus Apostolis and John Gregoropulus, both later to become prolific scribes. Among Lorenzo's active scribes was Caesar Strategus, prominent in the production of Torriano's *pulcherrimi*. The Florentine Studio was at the time under the supervision of Demetrius Chalcondyles, and one of the teachers, Janus Lascaris, became a lifelong friend of Musurus. Sometime after the exile of the Medici in 1494 Marcus traveled to Venice[1] and became Aldus Manutius' most important editor in the printing of Greek texts. At the very end of the fifteenth century Musurus went to the court of Alberto Pio at Carpi where he oversaw a sizeable library. In 1503 Marcus succeeded his old teacher Chalcondyles in the chair of Greek at Padua. The university was at this time very closely associated with the city of Venice, so, when the War of the League of Cambrai threatened in 1509, the school was closed and Musurus returned to the Serenissima. He was given a position teaching Greek and was awarded a modest stipend by the city. Musurus at the same time opened his house for private instruction and quickly resumed his close ties with the Aldine Press. With the ascension in 1513 of Lorenzo de' Medici's son Giovanni to the papal throne as Leo X, Marcus was soon persuaded by the pope and by Janus

---

[1] The time for Musurus' departure for Venice from Florence has traditionally been set in 1494. With the discovery that the Torriano *pulcherrimi* were not produced until 1494 and later we should probably push this move back to at least 1495. This will also affect dating of manuscripts copied from *pulcherrimi*. See, for example, Mark L. Sosower, "Marcus Musurus and a Codex of Lysias," *Greek, Roman, and Byzantine Studies* 23 (1982): 377–92, here 382–84.

Lascaris to assist in the establishment of a Greek College at Rome by locating young Greeks, forbidden by the Turks to study their ancestral culture, to bring to the West. Musurus left for Rome late in 1516. Planning to teach for a while in the College, then return to Venice and rejoin his own students there, Musurus died suddenly at Rome in October of 1517.[2]

Let us turn now to the suggestion that Marcus Musurus once owned the manuscripts referred to here as the *pulcherrimi*. Elpidio Mioni and Martin Sicherl[3] both independently and contemporaneously discovered that dedications contained in the front of several of these codices were written by Marcus Musurus. The dedications were directed to members of distinguished families and to well-known individuals from Venice and nearby places. Both Mioni and Sicherl concluded that, since Musurus had the power to dedicate the volumes, he must also have owned them. Both also agreed, and were supported by biographical data dealing with the dedicatees, that these expensive parchment manuscripts could have been acquired by Musurus only late in his life, during the time he was teaching at Venice, after the closure of the University of Padua. The manuscripts could, it was supposed, have been gifts of the families whose sons were being educated by Musurus or of friends who were ready to assist Musurus in establishing his own school. Mioni took the dedications to be indications that the manuscripts were awarded as prizes to outstanding students, but that they remained in the school when the students graduated, eventually being left with Musurus' friend Carlo Capella along with Marcus' other books when he went to Rome in 1516. While avoiding this part of the history, Sicherl, like Mioni, felt that the eventual arrival of the books at Saints John and Paul was owing to the legacy of the Dominican Girolamo Vielmi (d. 1583) who has, along with Gioachino Torriano, traditionally been cited as an important patron of the library.[4]

---

[2] For more on the life of Musurus and his importance for the transmission of Greek literature to the later Renaissance, see Legrand, *Bibliographie hellénique*, 1: CVIII-CXXIV, and 2: 312–21, 394–404; and Deno John Geanakoplos, *Greek Scholars in Venice* (Cambridge, MA, 1962), 111–66. See also Mioni, "La biblioteca greca di Marco Musuro," and Sicherl, "Musuros-Handschriften." Recently discovered documents are cited and incorporated into a life of Musurus recently published by A. Cataldi Palau, "La vita di Marco Musuro alla luce di documenti e manoscritti," *Italia medioevale e umanistica* 45 (2004): 295–369.

[3] Mioni, "La biblioteca greca di Marco Musuro," and Sicherl, "Musuros-Handschriften."

[4] In 1770, while tracing the origins of the library at Saints John and Paul, D.M. Berardelli ("Catalogus" [1770], 164) says: ". . . maximam horum Codicum cum Latinorum, tum Graecorum partem, eorum maxime, quorum rariora exstant exemplaria, aut elegantiori forma venustantur, ab Joachimo Turriano Veneto, ejusdem Caenobii alumno, Viro temporis sui longe doctissimo . . . summa cura, magnisque impensis collectam fuisse . . . Plures etiam Dominum Hieronymum Vielmium, ejusdem & ipsum Caenobii Alumnum, Episcopum prius Argolicensem, deinde Aemoniensem, vel donasse, vel

Other conclusions of Mioni and Sicherl, in addition to that concerning ownership, are shown by the Marcon lists to be equally untenable. Both Torriano's own list and the de Rachaneto list from the first years of the sixteenth century show that the *pulcherrimi* were being produced during Torriano's lifetime and that production ceased with his death. It therefore cannot be maintained that the manuscripts were produced in the second decade of the sixteenth century, thereby extending the period of Caesar Strategus' scribal activity into that period.[5] The supposed influence of Girolamo Vielmi, at least upon the Greek section of the Zanipolo library, was minimal (see Chapter IX). Because Marcus Musurus did not own the *pulcherrimi*, one cannot, as Mioni did, use bindings similar to those of the *pulcherrimi* or shared internal notations or scribal hands found also in other Zanipolo manuscripts as evidence of Musurus' ownership. Composite manuscripts, which the A and B lists show were independent, unbound volumes early in the sixteenth century, cannot be used to establish cooperative scribal undertakings between two different scribes. In spite of these objections, it would be unjust to minimize the scholarly efforts of Sicherl and Mioni, especially in researching the lives of the dedicatees and coming to the valid conclusion that Musurus' writing of the dedications and his final involvement with the *pulcherrimi* should be dated to the second decade of the 1500s.

The following list of dedications includes a brief rendition of the most important information about the dedicatees. Readers interested in more detailed information and the sources for that information should look to Mioni and Sicherl. The manuscripts with dedications number twenty:

Marc. IV, 8–   dedicated to Lorenzo Priuli, patrician, who died in 1559 at age 89.

Marc. IV, 10– dedicated to Antonio, son of Alvise Mocenigo, knight, patrician, and senator. Antonio died in 1558.

Marc. IV, 26– dedicated to Giovanni Cornaro, whose father George was the brother of Catarina, queen of Cyprus. Giovanni died in 1551.

Marc. IV, 29– dedicated to Nicola Sagundino, secretary to the Venetian Senate (d. 1551). Mioni dates his holding the position of secretary to the years 1511–1514 and thus provides us with our first firm dating of the dedications. Sicherl passed over this manuscript in the body of "Musuros-Handschriften," but accounted for it in a *Postskriptum* (601), after a communication from Mioni.

---

legasse . . ." Vielmi's part in the formation of the Zanipolo library will be investigated in Chapter VI below. Berardelli's statement would, however, appear to have played a large part in influencing Mioni's and Sicherl's opinions.

[5] Cataldi Palau, "La vita di Marco Musuro," 315, shows that by Musurus' own testimony Caesar Strategos was dead by 10 March 1498.

Marc. V, 4–	dedicated to Gaspare Contarini, patrician.
Marc. V, 5–	dedicated to Antonio Brocardo, son of the physician Marino. Antonio died young in 1531.
Marc. VII, 6–	dedicated to Bertucci Soranzo, patrician. In his catalogue Mioni identified Bertucci as a patrician who died in 1480. In "La biblioteca greca di Marco Musuro," 15, he changed the identification to another Bertucci Soranzo employed by Egidio of Viterbo in 1519.
Marc. VII, 7–	dedicated to Girolamo Zeno, patrician, who died in 1551 and was buried at Zanipolo. See also Marc. XI, 13 below.
Marc. VII, 8–	dedicated to Giovanni Abramio. This is the name of a Corfiote family visited by Janus Lascaris in 1491 while hunting for manuscripts for Lorenzo the Magnificent.[6] The dedication was lost in later binding. Both Mioni and Sicherl depended upon an old transcription by Morelli.
Marc. VII, 9–	dedicated to Antonio Marsilio, apparently a grown man and not a student of Musurus at this time.
Marc. VIII, 6–	dedicated to Paolo and Ladislao Priuli, teenagers at the time.
Marc. VIII, 7–	dedicated to Urbano [Bolzanio], Franciscan priest and teacher (died 1524).
Marc. VIII, 10–	dedicated to Marino Grimani, bishop of Ceneda and nephew of Domenico Cardinal Grimani. Marino became bishop of Ceneda in 1508.
Marc. IX, 5–	dedicated to Giovan Andrea, Girolamo, and Perino, sons of the patrician and senator Taddeo Contarini.
Marc. IX, 8–	dedicated to Marco Musuro of Crete, public school teacher.
Marc. IX, 10–	dedicated to Giacomo Semitecolo, already active in Venetian political life in 1516.
Marc. X, 1–	dedicated to Alvise Bembo, friend of Musurus. See Marc. XI, 14 below.
Marc. XI, 12–	dedicated to Alessandro da Bergamo, priest.
Marc. XI, 13–	dedicated to Girolamo Zeno, patrician. See Marc. VII, 7 above.
Marc. XI, 14–	dedicated to Alvise Bembo. See Marc. X, 1 above.

Now that the idea that Marcus Musurus once owned the *pulcherrimi* of the library at Saints John and Paul at Venice has been disposed of, it is not out of place to suggest a likely reason for his having written dedications on guard leaves

---

[6] For important information on the Abramius family of Corfu, see Basile Markesinis, "Janos Lascaris, la bibliothèque d'Avramis à Corfu et le Paris. gr. 854," *Scriptorium* 54 (2000): 302–6 and D. F. Jackson, "Janus Lascaris on the Island of Corfu in A.D. 1491," *Scriptorium* 57 (2003): 137–39.

of these volumes. The situation in which Musurus found himself when he was forced to leave Padua and set himself up in Venice as a public and private teacher of Greek suggests an explanation. Around 1510 Venice had no public library. Cardinal Bessarion's library was intended for public use, but it was still sequestered behind a partition in the Palace of the Doges, awaiting the long-promised library of St. Mark to be constructed.[7] The agreement to situate the Marciana at Zanipolo had fallen through. A remarkable library for scholars and general readers was to be opened at San Antonio di Castello, but not until after the death of its patron, Domenico Grimani, in 1523. Venice's small monastic collections were intended to serve the religious communities in which they were found, along with instructors already on stipend from the Venetian Senate who gathered their students together in these religious venues. A poor teacher with few books of his own would naturally have been drawn to Zanipolo and its Greek texts. These were stored in the desks which belonged to the city of Venice, Marcus' employer. He was well acquainted with the books from his own involvement in Torriano's *pulcherrimi* project along with his friends from Florence, Aristobulus Apostolis and Caesar Strategus. The Zanipolo manuscripts were an obvious resource for Musurus.

One deterrent to the use of the folio parchment manuscripts as teaching aids would have been their unbound state. Loose quires or quires collected within cardboard folders were unsuitable for classroom use or reading assignments, and such use would be harmful to the beautiful manuscripts themselves. Once bound, however, their clear script and variety of content would be ideal for teaching purposes. It appears that Musurus financed the binding of one volume himself and had prominent individuals finance the binding of others. The remainder were bound by the parents of students who would be using the texts. To make the expenditure more appealing to donors, he was careful in each dedication placed upon new guard leaves to praise adult donors or the students and their parents. The dedications certainly went beyond the twenty now extant and included other unbound manuscripts, even beyond the *pulcherrimi* group to others whose content was useful in Musurus' course of instruction. Rebinding in later centuries no doubt resulted in the loss of some old guard leaves and their dedications, especially in the case of manuscripts which left Venice. Torriano's codices now in libraries outside Venice were all later rebound and no dedications have been reported in them.

From what has been presented in this chapter and the preceding, the history of Gioachino Torriano's *pulcherrimi* and the rest of his collection can be traced with confidence down to the time of Marcus Musurus' departure for Rome in 1516. During the ten years before he made his bold proposal to the Venetian Senate Torriano accumulated a large number of Greek manuscripts,

---

[7] For an important account of the situation of the sequestered Bessarion manuscripts, see Lowry, "Two Great Venetian Libraries in the Age of Aldus Manutius."

many having belonged formerly to John Argyropulus. At the time of his proposal to found the Biblioteca Marciana at San Zanipolo Torriano began production of his *pulcherrimi*, probably to assure that the contribution of the Dominicans would not be dwarfed by the more substantial collection of Cardinal Bessarion when the library opened. But over the last years of Torriano's life he acquired other manuscripts in various sizes, many on paper, from various places, at the same time that the *pulcherrimi* were being written at Florence and Rome. After Torriano's death the whole collection was maintained at Zanipolo, and de Rachaneto's supplementary inventory, made early in the sixteenth century, attempted to account for everything missing from Torriano's own list. Little more seems to have been done with the collection for some time. The planned illumination and binding of the finer codices did not go forward. Although binding was complete in 1528 (see Richter below), no sign of it appears in de Rachaneto's inventory. It therefore seems likely that this binding was accomplished soon after 1510 through the efforts of Marcus Musurus, who may well have carried out his duties as a public instructor at San Zanipolo.

Whatever Musurus deposited with Carlo Capello when he went to Rome did not include the *pulcherrimi*. Nor did this group pass into other private hands. As will be shown below, they were still in place in 1528 and in the 1530s. Slow, steady dispersion did soon begin as several individual manuscripts slipped away. But the idea that they were all in the hands of Girolamo Vielmi, or that he recovered them so as to return them to their proper place, will soon be shown to be equally untenable.

VI. Martin Richter's List

During a visit to Venice in 1528 the German scholar Martin Richter compiled a list of Greek manuscripts maintained at three different places in the city. His findings are today contained in Vaticanus lat. 14011. These notes begin with the books of Cardinal Bessarion, based upon a list made in 1524 by Andreas Navagero, named *bibliotecario* of that collection in 1515. The other two sections of his notes include books he found at Saints John and Paul (fols. 15–17) and at S. Antonio di Castello (fols. 18–31). Some conclusions can be drawn about the Zanipolo notes based upon those which surround them. Richter dated his S. Antonio notes to October of 1528, before he moved on to Vienna and various collections in Austria. There is no reason to doubt that the Bessarion and Zanipolo lists were compiled around the same time. It is certain that Richter was not committed to making a complete inventory of manuscripts in the three Venetian repositories. While reasonably complete, the notes are often silent about duplicate copies of some works, and about grammars and frequently-encountered religious texts. Also, because his inventory of Bessarion books is admittedly derivative and because his descriptions of items at S. Antonio are simple reproductions of descriptions we find in the inventories of Cardinal Domenico Grimani,[1] it is clear that Richter's interests were mainly bibliographical. Unlike Gesner (below), Richter offers only one observation on physical aspects of the volumes he lists. It is thus reasonable to assume that his source for knowledge of books at Zanipolo was an in-house list of possessions which no longer exists, that he had first-hand knowledge of few volumes.

Richter's list shows that the Greek manuscripts of Zanipolo had by 1528 been arranged in the library by genre and were divided among eight desks provided by the Senate of Venice (see Chapter IV). It is also clear that most of the texts which were listed as unbound in previous inventories were bound by 1528 in much the same form as we see them today.[2] The following is the previously

---

[1] See Diller, Saffrey, and Westerink, *Bibliotheca Graeca*.

[2] A few examples of manuscripts existing independently on previous lists, but which had been brought together under one cover by 1528, are: Marc. IV, 8 (Marcon A 123 and A 128 = Richter 58), Marc. VIII, 7 (Marcon B 75 and A148 = Richter 64), and Marc. XI, 3 (Marcon A 149 and B89 = Richter 91). The first two of these are made up of Torriano *pulcherrimi*. That the previously unbound *pulcherrimi* were bound by 1528 aids in confirming the earlier suggestion that Marcus Musurus saw to their binding.

unpublished Richter Zanipolo list from Vat. lat. 14011, provided here with Arabic numerals to aid in easy reference and with cross-references to our other lists:

Libri Graeci ad Ioannem et Paulum Venetiis

1. *Biblia usque ad Ruth: cum Doctorum Glossatis* = B 67. See Gesner 20.
2. *Psalterium cum Variorum Doct: Expositione* = B 59, Gesner 21.
3. *Chrisost. Exameron* = B 70 = Marc. II, 4.
4. *Commentaria in Job: incerti authoris* = B 65.
5. *Basilius sup. Esaiam* = B 62 = Paris. gr. 495.
6. *Evangelium Mathaei cum variorum Doctorum expositione* = B 68.
7. *Eusebius de Preparatione Evangel.* = A 141 = Paris. gr. 466.
8. *Chris. homiliae* = B 71 = Marc. II, 182.
9. *Commentaria super Gregorium Naz.* Gregory Nazianzen is not mentioned by name on any of our other lists.
10. *Epistolae Basilii et variorum* = Marc. XI, 5. Pasted to the cover of this volume is an old label: *Basilii et Aliorum Epistolae*. On the pastedown is: *Epistolae Gregorii Nazianzeni et quaedam Basilii 400. annorum*. This was apparently written by Bernard de Montfaucon when he visited San Zanipolo on two occasions in 1698. Similar notes appear in several other manuscripts. The text begins abruptly with a Josephus fragment, to the right of which is written: *epte Basilii et aliorum multorum*. Epistles of Gregory Nazianzen begin under a clear title in a new hand on folio 5r. Medica which follow the epistles are first mentioned by Tomasini (number 69). There is a monocondylion on folio 91v which I decipher partially as 'Konstantinos . . . . . . nostos.' An apparently fifteenth-century hand wrote at the end of the manuscript that it contains Γαληνοῦ τὸ περὶ χρισήμων μετ' ἐπιστολῶν τοῦ γρηγορίου τοῦ θεο[λόγου], a good indication that the composite codex has been in its present form for a long time. Why Marc. XI, 5 is not found on our A or B lists is a mystery, perhaps explainable as de Rachaneto taking *Liber epistolorum* to be *Liber epitaphiorum*, as at A95.
11. *Epistolae Sinesii Episcopi* = B 31.

In Secundo Pulpito

12. *Varii Libri Galeni*. These first two Richter items seem to refer to loose quires of medica identifiable as works of Galen, but of unrecognized content. In Chapter V above the binding of some Zanipolo manuscripts was discussed. Of the medical volumes only Marc. V, 4 and V, 5 were there shown to be unbound. Our A and B lists tell us that Marc. V, 8 was already bound. Marc. V, 7 and V, 9 may or may not have been bound. Marc. V, 6 and Paris.

2153 were unbound. The state of Marc. XI, 5 is unclear. Another clearly unbound volume is the unidentified item at A 154.

13. *Galenus de Compositione Medicinarum.* = A 88 = Marc. V, 7.
14. *Galenus in Aphor: Hippocratis et ipsius quaedam alia* = Marc. V, 5 or V, 9, both of which today begin with this treatise.
15. *Galenus de Pulsib: et ipsius quaedam alia* = B 55 = Paris. 2153, fols. 47–169, followed by *De urinis.*
16. *Alexand: Trallianus in Medicina.* = B 55 = Marc. V, 9, fols. 236 ff.
17. *Galenus de Criticis ad Glauconem et Dioscorides* = B 32 = Marc. V, 8. This volume begins with Dioscorides-Oribasius, but with no reference to either author. Above a note on folio 1r declaring this to be a gift of Gioachino Torriano is another labeling the text *de crisibus sive diebus criticis*. In fact, *De crisibus* begins on folio 10r, *De diebus criticis* on folio 62r. Richter appears to have discovered his error in following the faulty note and made up for it with the next item (18). Dioscorides is named at folio 137v and more excerpts end the manuscript.
18. *Galenus de Crisib:* = B 32. See item 17 above.
19. *Galenus de Simplicii Medicina.* = A 105 = Marc. V, 6.
20. *Galeni Terapeutica.* = B 55 = Paris. 2153, folio 176, the first of a quire with the title: Γαληνοῦ πρὸς Γλαύκωνα· θεραπευτικῶν βιβλίον α′. Torriano clearly owned Vaticanus Reg. gr. 174 which has on a front guard leaf: *Mag^{ri} Ioachini pr. Venet. gene.* This manuscript of Galen's *Therapeuticae Methodus* cannot be shown to have resided in Venice, however. See Bibliothecae Apostolicae codices manuscripti . . . *Reginae Suecorum et Pii pp. II* . . ., H. Stevenson, Jr. recensuit, Rome 1888.
21. *Galeni quaedam opuscula.* Several opuscula not accounted for above occur in various places in our manuscripts
22. *Galenus in Prognost: Hippocratis* = Marc. V, 5 appears to be the only one of our identified manuscripts which contains this work (fol. 145). If it was bound by Richter's time, his going deep into the interior of the volume would be unusual. It is more likely that another Zanipolo manuscript which began with this work wandered from the collection. There are a few candidates still extant. Perhaps the most attractive is Escorial Φ-III-7 which once belonged to Don Hurtado de Mendoza, Spanish ambassador to Venice when Gesner visited in the 1530s.
23. *Quatuor Commentarii Procli in Euclidem. Catoptrica Euclidis. Phenomena Euclidis. Optica Euclidis. Datomena Euclidis.* = B 51 = Paris. 2532. Richter did not completely understand the title of Paris. 2352. It states that Proclus' commentary is on Book One of *Elementa* in four books.
24. *Joannes Grammaticus in Nicomachi Arithmeticam* = B 50 (q.v.)

25. *Quaedam Opera, quorum tituli secunda facie sextae paginae.*[3] This item must be a mathematical text, to judge by the items which surround it. One such manuscript which has not been identified is found on the Lascaris list at number 2 and, on the A list, number 150 probably also had a mathematical content.
26. *Euclidis Perspectiva. Nicomachi Arith:* This is also a possible identification for A150, just mentioned.

In Tertio Pulpito

27. *Platonis Opera* = B 1 = Marc. IV, 1.
28. *Platonis quaedam opera* = B 2.
29. *Plotini Enneades. Plotini Vita, authore Porphirio* = B 46 = Paris. 1970.
30. *Maximi Tyrii Platonici Opuscula* = A143 = Ambros. R 25 sup.
31. *Commentaria in Priora Aristotelis* = B 85 = Ambros. R 25 sup.
32. *Sexti Empirici communes Sententiae* = A 133 = Marc. IV, 26.
33. *Siriani solutiones Quest: Aristotelis in tertio Metaphisicae* = A 136 = Montpellier 120.
34. *viii Libri de Phisica auscultatione* = B 35 = Marc. IV, 4.
35. *Joannis Grammat: commenta: in iiii Phis: Aristotelis* = B 40 = Marc. IV, 20.
36. *Simplicii Commentaria in pr: & secundum Phis: Aristotelis* = B 36 = Marc. IV, 15.
37. *Simplicii commentaria in reliquos vi* = B 37–39 = Marc. IV, 16–18.
38. *Aristo: de Caelo et Mundo, De Gener: & Corrup: De Anima* = B 91 = Berlin Fol. 67 (?).
39. *Simplicius in iiii Libros de Caelo et Mundo* = B 58 = Paris. 1910.

In Quarto Pulpito

40. *Alexand: Aphrodisiensis in iiii libros Metheororum* = B 41 = Marc. IV, 6.
41. *Aristo: de Genera: animalium et de Partib:* = B 48 = Marc. IV, 24.
42. *Galeni Quaedam opera. Et Mischionis* = B 55 = Paris. 2153, fols. 218r-289v. This seldom-found work of Moschion follows various treatises of Galen in a manuscript once owned by Jean Hurault de Boistaillé. This part of the codex was written by a hand different from those which precede and follow; quire numbering is new, and its paper is different. As it is now, the volume does not mention Moschion, but circumstances early in the sixteenth century must have been different. Gesner also saw the manuscript

---

[3] My thanks to Dr. Antonio Manfredi of the Vatican Library for looking into this item for me. My photographs of Richter's list were not decipherable at this point.

and attributed the work to Moschion (number 11). A late hand on folio 220r identified the author as Soranus.[4]

43. *Simplicius in Libros de Anima* = B 42 = Marc. IV, 19.
44. *Alex: Aphrod: de Sensu et Sensato. Michaelis Ephesii in parva natural: Aristotelis* = A 134 = Parisinus gr. 1882.
45. *Aristot: et Theophrasti parva Animalia* = B 57 = Paris. 1921.
46. *Alex: Aphrod: iiii Libri, quorum duae habent questiones naturales, duae Ethica. Eiusdem de Fato. Commentarius ad Serenum et Antoninum. Galeni Diffinitiones Medicinae* = A 126 = Marc. IV, 10.
47. *Dionysius De Situ Orbis cum Commentario Eustachii Et Simplicius in Enchiridion Epicteti* = A 138 = Marc. XI, 13.
48. *Blemidis Epitome Philosophiae* = B 28 & A 156 = Vat. Barb. 246.
49. *Logotheti Opera* = B 6 = Paris. 2003.
50. *Theodori et Themistii Quaedam opuscula* = B 90 = Marc. XI, 18.
51. *Jo: Grammatici contra Proclum, de Mundi aeternitate.* This is the only reference to such a volume on our lists. There are few manuscript witnesses to this work.[5] Among possible identifications one stands out: Parisinus gr. 2058 was, like several other San Zanipolo volumes, acquired by Jean Hurault de Boistaillé at Venice through the services of Andreas Darmarius. The manuscript has a three-line, unfortunately illegible, *ex libris* on folio 1r.
52. *Sinesius De Somniis cum Commentariis* = B 49 = Marc. XI, 9.
53. *Paraphrasis incerti authoris in v. pr: Libros Ethicae Aristotelis* = B 44 = Marc. IV, 21. *Eiusdem in Residuos v.* = B 45 = Marc. IV, 22.
54. *Dionis Chrisostomi in Philosophia Morali* = B 53.

In Quinto Pulpito

55. *Logica Aristotelis cum Commentariis* = B 4.
56. *Ammonii ars Vetus* = A 130 = Marc. IV, 12.
57. *Simplicius in Praedicamenta Aristotelis* = B 34 = Marc. IV, 14.
58. *Alex: Aphrod: in Libros Priorum, Topicorum, Elenchorum* = A 93, A 123, A 132 = Marc. IV, 7, IV, 8, and IV, 9.
59. *Nicephori Logica* = Did Richter mistake Nicetas (David) for Nicephorus? See B33.
60. *Quaedam in Rhetorica. Tres orationes Eschinis. Apollonii de Constructione. Epistolae Phalaridis* = B 56 = Marc. VIII, 2.

---

[4] For a very good discussion of the Moschion-Soranus question see Alain Touwaide, review of P. Burguière et al., eds., *Soranus d' Éphèse, Maladies des femmes* (Paris, 1988), *Scriptorium* 44 (1990): 244*-45*.

[5] See *Philoponus De Aeternitate Mundi Contra Proclum*, ed. H. Rabe (Leipzig, 1899; repr. Hildesheim, 1963), III-XIII.

61. *Orationes Libanii* = B 22 = Marc. VIII, 9.
62. *Orationes Lysiae* = A 139 = Marc. VIII, 1.
63. *Commentum in Hermogenis Rhetoricam* = B 21 = Marc. XI, 2.

In Sexto Pulpito

64. *Aristidis Orationes* = B 75 and A 148 = Marc. VIII, 7.
65. *x Rhetores* = A 122 = Marc. VIII, 6.
66. *Juliani Imperatoris Orationes* = A 125.
67. *Demosthenis Orationes* = B 10 = Marc. VIII, 3.
68. *Demosthenis Orationes & Eschinis* = B 11 = Marc. VIII, 4.
69. *Dionysii Alicarnasei Methodi Rhetoricales et Soborati de componendis Declamationib: Varia Genera Declamationum* = B 86 = Marc. VIII, 10.
70. *Alexandri res Gestae per Arianum, Polyaeni Stratagemata* = A 118 = Marc. VII, 9.
71. *Appianus* = A 158 = Marc. VII, 10.
72. *Polibius* = A 119 = Marc. VII, 4.
73. *Dionysius Alicarnaseus* = A 135 = Marc. VII, 6.
74. *Tucidides* = B 7 and 8 = Marc. VII, 5 and Paris. suppl. 255.
75. *Chronica Georgii* = B 73 = Marc. VII, 12.
76. *Vitae Plutarchi* = B 20 = Marc. IV, 55.

In Septimo Pulpito

77. *Diodori Siculi v. Libri Primi. Eiusdem xx a sexto ad xx* = A 117 = Marc. VII, 7–8.
78. *Hesiodi Theogonia cum annotationibus Hesiodi, Aspis Heraclis, Erymna soluta. Phurnuti orationes. Opus Palephati De non credendo historiis. In Hesiodi Theogoniam Comment: Hesiodi opera et Dies, Theogonia cum Commentariis* = A137 = Marc. IX, 6. Pertusi says that the *Theogony* scholia come from Vaticanus gr. 38 which was in its present location when Musurus copied it. See A. Pertusi, "La tradizione manoscritta degli scolii alle *Opere e Giorni* e le note inedite attribuite a Massimo Planude," *Studi bizantini e neoellenici* 7–8 (1953): 177–82, here 179.
79. *Commentarii super Iliadem* = A 124 = Marc. IX, 5.
80. *Euripides cum annotationib:* = B 19 = Marc. IX, 12.
81. *Euripidis Tragodiae aliquot* = B 18 = Marc. IX, 11.
82. *Eglogae Stobaei* = A 131 = Marc. IV, 29.
83. *Pindarus integer cum annotationibus* = A 121 = Marc. IX, 8.
84. *Eustachii narratio lepidissima de Hismeno & Hismenia. Herodiani de Caesaribus, Dionysii de Structura Orationis, collocationeque Verborum* = A 144, A 120 = Marc. XI, 14.

85. *Suidas* = B 9 = Marc. XI, 8.
86. *Lexicon Graecum & Latinum* = B 15 –17 = Marc. X, 17 and ?
87. *Julii Pollucis Vocabularium. Duo Tragodiae Aeschili. Dionysius de Situ Orbis. Theocriti Eglogae aliquot* = B 12 = Marc. XI, 7.

In Octavo Pulpito

88. *Athanasius.* Athanasius is mentioned on several of our lists, but usually among Latin texts. Number 223 on Marcon's B list, *Athanasius contra Gentes,* is identified as Marc. lat. II, 2. Tomasini on page 27 places this among Latin texts. For more information we have Bernard de Montfaucon, *Bibliotheca bibliothecarum* (Paris, 1739), 479: *Ambrosii Camaldulensis versio libri Athanasii contra Gentes & de Incarnatione.* There was a Greek Athanasius lexicon (see Gesner, number 2 below) at San Zanipolo (= Marcon B 13), however, and it is that to which Richter must be referring here. See also Vielmi, number 1, in Chapter VIII.1 below.
89. *Clementis Opera* = A 140 = Marc. XI, 4.
90. *Liber Georgicorum e Variis Utriusque Linguae authoribus. Stephanus de Urbibus* = A 127 = Marc. XI, 12.
91. *Magnum Ethimologicum. Opus Platonis de legibus* = A 149 = Marc. XI, 3.
92. *Apollonius Grammaticus. Ephestio de Carminibus Opusculum in Progymnasmata* = A 129 = Marc. X, 1.
93. *Grammatica Theodori* = B 26 = Marc. X, 11.
94. *Institutiones Grammaticae* = B 25 = Marc. X, 6.
95. *Emanuelis Grammatica et alia quaedam* = B 29 = Marc. X, 5.
96. *Moscopoli declarationes Vocabulorum* = B 24 = Marc. X, 3.
97. *Epistolae Phalaridis* = B 14 = Marc. VIII, 11.
98. *Procopii de aedificiis Constantinopolis Arpocrationis de Distinctionib: Oratorum* = A 146 = Geneva Bodmer 43 (158).
99. *Imagines Philostrati et quaedam Epigrammata* = B 23 = Marc. XI, 15.
100. *Definitiones et Epistolae Platonis* = B 3 = Marc. IV, 2.
101. *Liber quidam Arabicus.*

VII. Conrad Gesner and San Zanipolo

In preparation for his monumental *Bibliotheca universalis* (Tiguri, 1545–1549) Conrad Gesner visited Italian libraries in Rome, Bologna, Florence, and Venice. Among manuscripts he saw in Venice he refers often to those of Cardinal Bessarion, San Antonio di Castello, Saints John and Paul, and Diego Hurtado de Mendoza, mentioned in volume one as imperial ambassador to Venice and in later volumes as relocated to Rome. Gesner's main purpose in his publication was to compile an exhaustive list of Latin, Greek, and Hebrew writers and their works, as well as to list printed editions of the same. In the case of authors and works which had not yet been printed, he indicated where he had seen manuscript witnesses. Unfortunately, Gesner often gives only generalized locations, such as *in Italia* or *Venetiis*, but from time to time he does mention Zanipolo explicitly as a place where he saw specific texts during the 1530s. In his prefatory notes Gesner admits that library inventories were his main source of information, but it is also clear that he had eyewitness familiarity with certain manuscripts. These data, infrequent and limited as they are, are nonetheless useful for recognizing some codices which were still maintained at Zanipolo in the decade following Richter's visit and in helping to identify some manuscripts the descriptions of which in earlier inventories are insufficiently complete:

1. (*Bibliotheca universalis* 1:42v)—*Andronici scholia Graeca in Homerum Venetiis reservantur in bibliotheca SS. Ioannis & Pauli*. This intriguing item has not yet been satisfactorily explained. Gesner himself goes on to say: "Nimirum hic est ille M. Pompilius Andronicus Grammaticus desidiosior in possessione Graeca . . . ex urbe se Cumas contulit, ibique in ocio vixit . . ." Fabricius[1] was not persuaded of this identification: "Andronici scholia Graeca in Homerum MSta extitisse Venetiis in Bibliotheca SS. Johannis & Pauli, memorat Gesnerus in Bibl., etsi Thomasinus in Catalogo MSS Bibl. Venet. nullam ejus mentionem facit. Videtur autem Gesnero hic esse M. Pompilius Andronicus . . . conjectura ut mihi quidem videtur non valde verisimili." There is nothing in the Didymus commentary on Homer in Marc. IX, 5 to recommend attributing it to Andronicus (A 124 above). Gesner was familiar with Didymus on Homer (I: 204v-205r), but he did not mention the Zanipolo manuscript when writing about him. Perhaps the answer to

---

[1] Joannes Albertus Fabricius, *Bibliotheca graeca* (Hamburg, 1795), 1: 293.

this problem lies in another Homer commentary, the unidentified item B 88 above.

2. (1:98v)—*Athanasii Lexicon Graecum extat Venetiis in bibliotheca SS. Ioannis & Pauli.* = Marcon B 13, Richter 88. See Vielmi number 1 below.

3. (1:177r)—*Paedagogum Clementis Graece vidi Venetiis in bibliotheca SS. Ioan. & Pauli. Sunt autem tres libri per capita quaedam & tanquam loci communes distincti. Et quod valde doleo, capita quaedam, licet pauca, non sunt integra.* Clement is now part of the composite manuscript Marc. XI, 4–a *pulcherrimus*. Since Clement was not included on the A and B lists, this must have been a late delivery to the collection. = A140.

4. (1:188v)—*Cornuti brevis enumeratio τῶν κατὰ τὴν Ἑλληνικὴν θεωρίαν παραδεδομένων, extat Romae in Vaticana bibliotheca. Item liber de diis coelestibus, & Phornuti de diis gentilium: quare videtur alius esse Cornutus a Phurnuto, etsi quidam confundere soleant: sed nihil certi habeo.* = A137 (Marc. IX, 6). See number 14 below.

5. (1:208v)—*. . . in alio quodam nescio cuius Italicae Bibliothecae catalogo Dionis sermones 83. extare legi. Haec ipsa autem videntur esse opuscula illa, de quibus Raph. Volaterranus in Dione Cassio dixit:* (on this same page Gesner had just discussed Volaterranus' confusion of Cassius Dio and Dio of Prusa) *nec aliud esse puto volumen in philosophia morali huius authoris nomine Venetiis in bibliotheca SS. Io. & Pauli.* Marcon shared Volaterranus' confusion, so we should see her B 53 as Dio Chrysostom, but not necessarily containing anything like eighty-three orations.

6. (1:268r)—*Georgii cuiusdam Graeci monachi historia temporum sive chronica, a condito mundo usque ad regnum Nicephori Botaniatae, extat manu scripta Venetiis in bibliotheca SS. Ioannis & Pauli.* = B 73 = Marc. VII, 12.

7. (1:397r-v)—*Ioannis Cantacuzeni Imperatoris Constantinopolitani, qui assumpto monachi habitu IOASAPH monachus est cognominatus . . . Paraphrasis in quinque libros Ethicorum Aristotelis, servatur Graece Venetiis in bibliotheca SS. Ioannis & Pauli.* = B 44 = Marc. IV, 21.

8. (1:423r-v)—*Ioannis Grammatici Alexandrini, cognomine Philoponi . . . Liber de pulsibus.Commentarii in Arithmeticam Nicomachi Geraseni. In Astrolabium planum, alias de usu astrolabii. Commentarii in Elenchos Aristotelis, Venetiis in bibliotheca SS. Ioannis & Pauli.* How many of these works Gesner saw in Venice is not clear. We know that Nicomachus Gerasenus was among the authors at Zanipolo (Richter number 24). Philoponus' treatise on the astrolabe is found in Paris. 1921 (B57).[2] A Philoponus commentary on *Sophistici Elenchi* is not specifically attested elsewhere, but it may well be part of Marcon B 82 (q.v.).

---

[2] Ed. and intro. A.P. Segonds, *Traité de l'astrolabe* (Paris, 1981).

9. (1:469v)—*Iulianus princeps Romanus: Orationes quaedam eius custodiuntur Venetiis in bibliotheca SS. Ioan. & Pauli.* = A 125.
10. (1:509r)—*Maximus Tyrius philosophus... alias quaedam philosophicas quaestiones... Has quaestiones sive Sermones vel capita 41. Graece vidi Venetiis in bibliotheca SS. Ioan. & Pauli.* = A 143 = Ambros. R 25 sup.
11. (1:514r)—*Moschion, alias Mischion scripsit Graece de mulierum affectibus, quem librum Venetiis vidi in bibliotheca SS. Io. & Pauli, divisum in capita 167.* Gesner at I:601v lists Soranus on diseases of women, but he does not connect him with Moschion or report a manuscript of Soranus at Zanipolo. This is a good indication that the Soranus identification in Paris. 2153 (see Richter 42 above) was inserted after the late 1530s. The Paris manuscript has its own πίναξ τῶν γυναικῶν παθῶν beginning on folio 218r, items numbered through ρξδ′ (164), but the delta looks very much like zeta—thus leading to Gesner's error. Corresponding numbers in the text do not extend to the end, so no correction offered itself. = A 98 = Paris. 2153. For a good discussion of the names Moschion and Soranus see Touwaide, review of Burguière et al.
12. (1:516r)—*Blemmidae Epitomen philosophiae vidi Venetiis in bibliotheca SS. Io. & Pauli, manuscriptum volumen in folio, crassitudine circiter sesquidigitum.* = A 156 = Vatic. Barb. 246.
13. (1:561v)—*Philostrati Icones, Graece cum scholiis extant Venetiis in bibliotheca SS. Ioannis & Pauli manuscriptae.* = B23 = Marc. XI, 15.
14. (1:562v)—*Phurnutus, alias Phornutus, praenomine Polydeuces, scripsit opusculum de aerumnis Herculis, quod extat Graece Venetiis in bibliotheca SS. Ioannis & Pauli.* In speaking of the Aldine edition he adds: "capita sunt 35. in fine libri non Phurnutus, sed κορνοῦτος scribitur." See number 4 above, A 137 (Marc. IX, 6).
15. (1:569v–570r)—*Porphyrius. Liber de prosodia Graecus, servatur ibidem in bibliotheca SS. Ioannis & Pauli, manuscriptus in fol. chartis 4. & dimid.* = A140 = Marc. XI, 4.
16. (1:596v)—*Sexti empirici Sceptici sermones decem, alias Sceptica, sive contra omnes scientias. Opus Graecum satis magnum extat apud Diegum Hurtadum Caesaris oratorem Venetiis, & ibidem in bibliotheca SS. Ioannis & Pauli.* = A 133 = Marc. IV, 26.
17. (1:606v)—*Syriani solutiones quaestionum in tertio libro metaphysicorum Aristotelis, Venetiis extant Graece in biblioth. SS. Io. & Pauli.* = A136 = Montpell. 120. Although commentary on more books occurs in the Montpellier codex, its only title is reported by Omont[3] to refer uniquely to: Τὰ εἰς τὸ γ′ τοῦ Συριανοῦ τοῦδε...

---

[3] H. Omont, *Catalogue des manuscrits grecs des départements* (Paris, 1886), 45.

18. (2:46v) — *In Aristotelis Priora commentarii extant Venetiis in bibliotheca SS. Ioannis & Pauli, authore incerto, quorum initium est:* ὁ σκοπὸς τῆς παρούσης πραγματείας διαπεφώνηται. = B 85 = Ambros. R 25 sup.
19. (2.54v) — *Rhetorum decem orationes Venetiis extant in bibliotheca SS. Io. & Pauli.* = A 122 = Marc. VIII, 6.
20. (3.15r) — *Biblia Graeca cum commentariis sparsim collectis, extant Venetiis in Bibliotheca SS. Io. & Pauli.* = B 67.
21. (3.24v) — *Psalterium Graecum cum commentariis variorum authorum, volumen magnum, Venetiis in Bibliotheca SS. Ioannis & Pauli.* = B 59.

VIII. Girolamo Vielmi and the Zanipolo Library

The origins, shape, and size of the Greek manuscript collection at Saints John and Paul of Venice owed much to the assiduous activity and grand plan of Gioachino Torriano. Another name has traditionally been connected to the growth of the library, but with little hard evidence to support that tradition. This name is that of another former member of the Zanipolo community, Girolamo Vielmi (d. 1582), who went on to a life of distinction as a bishop and scholar.[1]

Vielmi's reputed connection with the growth of the Zanipolo library goes back to the inventory of Filippo Tomasini (see next chapter). At the end of his list of manuscripts maintained at Saints John and Paul of Venice, Tomasini added the following note:

> Multi Codices huius Bibliothecae arbitrantur fuisse D. Vielmi Episcopi Aemoniensis, qui obiit 1582. in hoc Coenobio, cuius Bibliothecam Sansovinus Venetiis inter alias recenset.

Berardelli, on page 167 of his catalogue of 1770, cited Tomasini and added:

> Plures (libros) etiam Dominum Hieronymum Vielmium, ejusdem & ipsum Caenobii Alumnum, Episcopum prius Argolicensem, deinde Aemoniensem, vel donasse, vel legasse, Thomasinus idem loco supra laudato arbitratur. Ejus certe Bibliothecam valde commendat Sansovinus in Opere *Venezia &c. descritta* sub titulo *Librarie*, pag. mihi 257. tergo, edit. 1604., eamque praestantioribus inter Venetas, dignioribusque adnumerat: qua proinde eo magis verisimile fit, Virum praeclarissimum voluisse Caenobium suum, in quo diem etiam obivit ultimum, pro sua benevola voluntate dictare.

The care that both Tomasini and Berardelli exercised here in treating the possibility that Vielmi had a great influence on the library at Saints John and Paul carried over into the opening lines of an important study of the collection by Rinaldo Fulin: "Lasciando pure da parte i codici latini e greci di Girolamo Vielmo..."[2]

---

[1] For reference materials related to the life and writings of Vielmi see Marcon, "Per la biblioteca a stampa," 246, n. 32.

[2] Fulin, "Vicende della libreria."

On the other hand, Mioni and Sicherl,[3] in their discussions of Marcus Musurus, assumed that Vielmi played a key role in the transmission especially of the *pulcherrimi*. It seems therefore worthwhile to investigate, as far as possible, how much influence Vielmi could have exerted on the development of the Greek library of Zanipolo.

There exists a formerly unpublished, notarized inventory of Vielmi's books which is of some use in such an investigation. The inventory, now in the Bibliotheca Apostolica Vaticana, is unfortunately terse in its descriptions, seldom indicates whether an item is a manuscript or an imprint, and seldom indicates the language of the text. Its first part consists of volumes Vielmi kept at his episcopal residence at the time of his death. The rest of the inventory was completed after that portion of the library had been transported to Venice. The second part consists of a collection of books Vielmi had in his studio at Zanipolo where he spent his last days away from his episcopal see.[4] The following is an extract from the inventory consisting of items which contain the names of Greek authors and which might be taken to be manuscripts.[5] This list is, then, only a small portion of the whole inventory, but it serves to demonstrate the actual effect Vielmi had on the Greek library at San Zanipolo:

Vaticanus lat. 3958, folios 133r-148v.
Die Veneris 23. mensis martii 1582.

Hoc est inventarium particulare librorum omnium qui fuerunt R.^{mi} bonae memoriae D. Hieronymi Vielmi, olim Episcopi Aemoniensis existentium in Monasterio Sanctorum Jo. et Pauli Venetiarum in studio proprio (?) R.^{mi} Epi., quorum pars e Civitate Aemoniensi una cum aliis rebus et bonis eiusdem R.^{mi} Ep^i. lesgato commissione Ill.^{mi} et R.^{mi} D. Legati Ap.^{i} Venetorum per me notarium et curiae suae scribam ad hoc deputatum huc transportata fuit, alia vero pars hic reperiebat, quod quidem Inventarium per me Notarium, et scribam infrascriptum factum fuit de speciali mandato prolibati Ill.^{mi} et R.^{mi} D. Legati Ep.^{i} et sequitur vz.

Infrascripti fuerunt transportati e Civitate Aemoniensi:

---

[3] See Mioni, "La biblioteca greca di Marco Musuro," 21; Sicherl, "Musuros-Handschriften," 600.

[4] This studio may well be the same as that mentioned in Marcon, "I libri del Generale Domenicano," 100, one in which visitors stayed and books were kept: "Libri sono in el studio sopra la scala dicono essere delo fiolo de misser Franguli greco in pegno per ducati tre."

[5] Greek authors and works listed on the inventory but accompanied by a place name and/or date are taken to be imprints and are therefore omitted from this excerpt.

1. *Lexicon Theologicon.* The two Greek words indicate the language of this volume, but whether it was a manuscript or an imprint is unclear. Both Richter (number 88) and Gesner (his number 2) cite a volume of Athanasius of Alexandria at Zanipolo, the latter calling it *Lexicon*—perhaps the volume Vielmi had with him.
2. *Joannis Crisostomi in Divi Pauli Epistolas.* Once again an unidentified Zanipolo manuscript may be spoken of here. At Marcon A 142 Chrysostom is mentioned with no reference to content. If this and that item are the same, the manuscript was a commentary of Chrysostom on the Pauline epistles (cf. CPG 4426–4440), on parchment, perhaps by a *pulcherrimi* scribe, but not necessarily.
3. *Beati Theodoreti in epistolas s.^{ti} Pauli.* This is probably the Latin edition of 1552 from Florence.
4. *Simplicius in Fisicam.* Marc. IV, 15–18, belonged to Gioachino Torriano (B 36–39), but the Marciana also owns an Aldus-Asulanus imprint from 1526 which can take its place among other possible candidates for this Vielmi volume.
5. *Alexandri quaestiones na(tura)les.* Marc. IV, 10 (Marcon A 126) is a possibility.
6. *Alexandri Afrodisiensis in libros Metheorologicorum.* Marc. IV, 6, belonged to Torriano (Marcon B 41).
7. *Alexandri Afrod. in priora Aristotelis.* Marc. IV, 7 ? (Marcon A 93).
    "Infrascripti fuerunt reperti in studio G.^{ti} et R.^{mi} D. Epi. in monasterio sanctorum Jo. et Pauli Venetiis."
8. *Euclides in artem Geometriae.* Torriano owned an *Elementa* (Marcon B 51), but it was gone from Zanipolo (= Paris. 2352) by this time. We are probably dealing with a Latin translation here. See Marcon B 149.
9. *Dicionarium Graecum cum Interpretatione Latina.* Torriano had three of these (Marcon B 15–17) and Marc. X, 17 remains.
10. *Porphirii de abstinentia ab esu animalium.* Tomasini (below) at page 26 lists a *Tractatus de Abstinentia . . . 4.m.*, a Latin text. Berardelli numbers 206–208[6] are parchment volumes of Nicolaus de Byart entitled *Summa de abstinentia*, one of them quarto size. It was probably this which Tomasini saw and listed. The Vielmi item is probably Jo. Bernardo Feliciano's Latin translation (*de Abstinentia ab esu animalium*) printed by Gryphius at Venice in 1547. There was a Greek text of the work printed at Florence in 1548, but Feliciano's title is persuasive.
11. *Dioscoride sopra il materiale.* There is no evidence of such a manuscript at San Zanipolo. This is probably an early imprint, of which there were several, most titled *De materia medica*.

---

[6] Berardelli, "Catalogus." His numbers 1–103 are in volume 32 (1778), 104–263 in 33 (1779), 264–392 in 35 (1780), 393–492 in 37 (1782), 493–548 in 38 (1783), 549–607 in 39 (1784), and 608–647 in 40 (1784).

12. *Epictetus graecus.* This could be Marc. XI, 13 (Marcon A 138).
13. *Serianus in xii libros Methafisicos.* This should not be mistaken for Marcon A136 which is regularly described as a commentary *in tertio libro*, today Montpellier 120, already gone from Zanipolo by 1582. Both Richter (number 33) and Gesner (number 17) cite Book Three as the text of the Montpellier codex. This is what the opening lines of the volume itself refer to. What the notary was looking at here is not at all clear.
14. *Claudi ptolomei Alexandrini Geograniae.* Berardelli 447 is a paper codex from the fifteenth century in 137 folios. He, like the notary of the Vielmi list, had trouble with the title of the work, each at the same place. Berardelli calls it *Claudii Ptolomei Alexandrini Geograghiae lib. VIII.* He says it was dated 24 December 1445 and was a Latin translation of Jacobus Angelus Florentinus.
15. *Almagies Tholomei.* There are several *Almagest* imprints which Vielmi may have owned. None, understandably, reproduces this fanciful title.
16. *Beati Theodoreti Episcopi Ciri.* Many works of Theodoret were available to Vielmi in Latin translation. Among the ones which mention his bishopric in their titles are *Beati Theodoreti Episcopi Cyri interpretatio in omnes Davidis Psalmos. Ab Antonio Carafa . . . conversa* (Padua: Gallastius, 1565) and *Theodoreti Episcopi Cyri Eranistes seu Polymorphus* (Venice: Farreus, 1548).
17. *Logica Aristotelis.* Both de Rachaneto (Marcon A 190) and Tomasini (page 27) use this title for a Latin translation which belonged earlier to Torriano. Berardelli at number 427 describes it in detail as a parchment folio of the fourteenth century, 147 folios: *Aristotelis Opera quaedam*, containing the complete *Organon*, and says that it had on the first page *Logica Aristotelis ex dono magistri Joachini Turriani Veneti, qui fuit Generalis.*
18. *Plutarchi libellus.* The A list offers two possible identifications for this item, A 82: *Problemata Plutarchi ut supra*, a Latin work, and A 101: *Plutarcho de institutione puerorum in greco non ligato.* Laurentianus 80.25 is offered above as a likely identification for that item. If that is the volume Vielmi had with him, his death will provide a *terminus post quem* for the Laurentian acquisition of the manuscript of 17 folios.
19. *Gieroglificha Apolinis.* There are several sixteenth-century imprints of Horapollo, usually employing various forms of the word *Hieroglyphica.*
20. *Historia Nicephori.* Apparently Marc. VII, 14, the history of Nicephorus Callistus Xanthopulus, a volume mentioned on none of these lists until Berardelli's. If it was a gift of Vielmi, it should be assumed that Tomasini omitted it from his inventory, a not unusual occurrence.
21. *Vitae de Plutarco.* Perhaps Marc. IV, 55, owned by Torriano (Marcon B 20).
22. *Ecclesiastica historia.* Probably the Latin text of Cassiodorus seen by Tomasini (his page 27). Berardelli at 553 calls it *Historia Ecclesiastica.*

23. *Eusebii Caesariensis.* See Marcon A 6 and A 12. Berardelli at number 560 reflects the wording of the A list: "Eusebii Pamphili Caesariensis E. Temporum liber seu Chronicon ab Abraamo . . ."
24. *Phylonis Judei.* Several imprints will fit here.
25. *Divi Gregorii nisenni in hexameron.* See Tomasini page 23: "Libri X. Moralium S. Gregorii, Etrusco idiomate, char. fol. Anno 1473. scripti."
26. *Amonis episcopi in Apocalypsim.* This is *Haymonis Episcopi Halberstattensis Commentariorum in Apocalypsim . . . libri VII* (Cologne, 1529).
27. *Textus Philosophiae Aristotelis.* Probably Marc. IV, 24, owned by Torriano (Marcon B 48). Several Latin philosophical works are also possibilities.
28. *Aristotelis de historia animalium.* This Latin translation is listed by Tomasini on page 28. Berardelli at number 429 uses the same title.
29. *Orationes divi Basilii.* This is probably one of the imprints listed as lost at the beginning of Berardelli's Latin list in 1779: "S. Basilii Magni opera, Parisiis 1518. Tom. 2."
30. *Epistolae Pauli latinae et graecae in uno Codice.*
31. *B.ti Jo. Damasceni contra opugnatores immaginum.* John Damascene wrote three orations against Iconoclasts, works found in few Greek manuscripts.[7] There is no reason to believe that Vielmi owned one of them. Nicolaus Majoranus published the Greek text at Rome in 1553, Godefridus Tilmannus at Paris in 1555.
32. *Diogenis Laerccii.* This could be Marc. IV, 15. Marcon, "Per la biblioteca a stampa" (239, number 35), points to a Jensen imprint of Diogenes Laertius at the Marciana dated 1475.

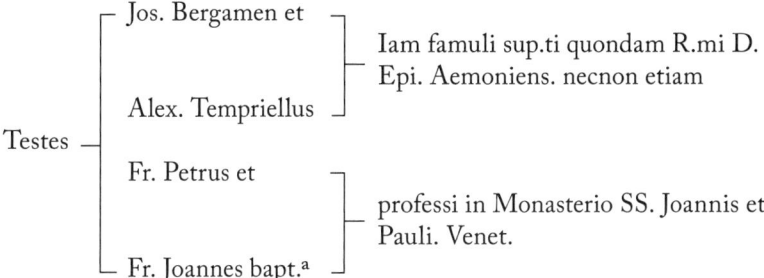

The list just now presented offers interesting and conclusive testimony about Girolamo Vielmi's connections with the Greek library of Saints John and Paul. He took to his episcopal residence at least three Greek manuscripts from the library (items 5, 6, and 7). He may have taken two others, as well (items 1 and 4). Four of the five items point to an interest in philosophical commentaries; the

---

[7] B. Kotter, ed., *Contra imaginum calumniatores tres,* Die Schriften des Johannes von Damaskos 3 (Berlin and New York, 1975), 34–39 lists the manuscripts, with Marc. II, 62 on 38.

fifth and least well attested is a theological lexicon. Item 5 (Marc. IV, 10) is one of the *pulcherrimi* and a philosophical text. It is noteworthy that the library allowed a *pulcherrimus* and former Argyropulus volumes to be removed from the site indefinitely, at the same time that others were being sold. Vielmi's former membership in the community and later ecclesiastical ascendancy no doubt gave him some freedom, but a general tendency toward carelessness also seems to have set in.

When Vielmi returned to the community for his last days, it appears he kept beside him at least four Greek manuscripts from the library (items 9, 12, 21, and 27). Two other items (18 and 32) are probably Zanipolo manuscripts. The content of none of these is out of keeping with Vielmi's earlier interests. Most noteworthy, however, is item 20, which appears on no list before Vielmi's inventory and could therefore be a single manuscript Zanipolo inherited from him. Because Tomasini did not see it and because the description is so unspecific, the possibility remains that this, like so many others, was a printed text. No matter which possibility is favored for item 20, the inevitable conclusion is that Girolamo Vielmi's influence upon the library of Saints John and Paul in the area of the Greek manuscripts was of no importance. His greatest gift to the collection may well have been his borrowing and holding on to several manuscripts at a time when many left Zanipolo and Venice, never to return.

IX. The Tomasini List

As part of his inventory of manuscripts in various places around the city of Venice in the mid-seventeenth century, Giovanni Filippo Tomasini[1] included the contents of the library at Saints John and Paul. He found Greek codices in plutei I, II, III, V, and VII in the section of the library designated *A parte dextera*. He listed seventy-eight Greek volumes, considerably fewer than even Richter had recorded in his selection of texts. This reduction in numbers indicates that many Greek manuscripts had left the collection between 1528 and 1650. Losses after 1650 were few, so Tomasini's list differs little in the numbers of Greek manuscripts attributable to San Zanipolo from those in the catalogue made by Berardelli in 1770, or in Mioni's recent catalogue. A couple of differences should be highlighted, however. One Plato volume (item 19 below) left the library between 1650 and 1770 and has not been identified. One volume of Thucydides was not returned from Paris after the Napoleonic Wars (item 73 below).[2]

Bibliotheca SS. Ioannis & Pauli Venetiis.

Supra ostium:

Viris Illustribus Condita Domus.
Libri Graeci.

Pluteus I:
A parte dextera.

1. *Orationes Aristidis, charactere antiquo. fol. membr.* = A148, B75 = Marc. VIII, 7.
2. *Suidae Lexicon. f.m.* = B9 = Marc. XI, 8.
3. *Magnum Etymologicum. eleganti charactere. fol. m.* = A149 = Marc. XI, 3 (pt. 1).
4. *Aeschinis Orationes. Apollonius de constructione. Phalaridis Epistolae. 8.m.* = B56 = Marc. VIII, 2.

---

[1] J.F. Tomasini, *Bibliothecae Venetae manuscriptae publicae et privatae* (Udine, 1650), 20–23 for the Greek manuscripts of Zanipolo.

[2] The manuscript lost in the removal of manuscripts to Paris is an 11th-or 12th-century parchment Thucydides codex which once belonged to Theodore Metochites. It is today Paris. suppl. gr. 255. In its place another Thucydides, today Marc. VII, 50, a former possession of the Jesuits of Paris, was sent to Venice.

5. *Hesiodi opera cum Scholiaste, variisq. lectionibus & notis. fol. membr.* = A137, A159 = Marc. IX, 6. Cornutus and the Labors of Hercules also appear in this volume, but Tomasini did not notice them. Later, at the end of the descriptions of Tomasini Pluteus VI, he reported that Gesner said that he saw Phurnutus and the Labors in the library. See Richter number 78.
6. *Stobaeus Eclogae. fol. m.* = A131 = Marc. IV, 29.
7. *Dionysius de situ Orbis. Epicteti Comment. Simplicii super Enchiridion. fol. m. Liber fuit Hieronymi Zeni Patricii Veneti.* = A138 = Marc. XI, 13.
8. *Simplicius in Praedicamenta Aristotelis. fol. chart.* = B34 = Marc. IV, 14.
9. *Simplicius in Primum & Secundum Physicorum. fol. chart.* = B36 = Marc. IV, 15.
10. *Simplicius in 3. & 4. Physicorum. fol. chart.* = B37 = Marc. IV, 16.
11. *Simplicius in 5. & 6. Physicorum. f. chart.* = B38 = Marc. IV, 17.
12. *Simplicius in 7. & 8. Physic. f. c.* = B39 = Marc. IV, 18.
13. *Simplicius in Lib. de Anima. f. c.* = B42 = Marc. IV, 19.
14. *Polybii Historia. charactere eleganti. fol. memb.* = A119 = Marc. VII, 4.
15. *Alexandri Aphrodisaei Quaestiones Naturales, & Scholia dubitationum Moralium & Solutionum Lib. IV. Idem ad Imperatores de Fortuna, & Fine nostro. Incipit: ἐν μὲν, etc. Definitiones Medicae Galeno adscriptae. fol. memb.* = A126 = Marc. IV, 10.
16. *Porphyrius in Categorias Arist. Aristotelis Analytica. Eiusdem Topica. charactere antiquo. memb. f.* = B5 = Marc. IV, 5.
17. *Georgii Cedreni Chronicum hoc titulo: Synopsis Chronicorum à fundatione Orbis usque ad Regnum Isaci Comneni, collecta ex diversis. fol. chart.* = B73 = Marc. VII, 12.
18. *Platonis opera.* = B 2. The other two Plato manuscripts Tomasini saw were parchment. This one must have been paper and = B 2.
19. *Alterum Platonis Vol. f. m.* = B 1. The only one of the three Plato manuscripts Tomasini saw which fits this description is Marc. IV, 1.
20. *Item Platonis opera. cuius initium est Timaeus. finis de Politica. f. m. eleganti & antiquo charactere.* This is not an item which appears on any of the other lists, nor does it seem to exist any longer. It must have been a late acquisition which departed from Zanipolo after 1650 and before Berardelli made his catalogue.

Pluteus II.

21. *Sextus Empiricus. in memb. f.* = A133 = Marc. IV, 26.
22. *Dionysius Halicarnassaeus. m. fol.* = A135 = Marc. VII, 6.
23. *Vocabularium Graecum latine Explicatum. chart. fol. Incipit:* Λεξικὸν ἀναγκαῖον, *&c.* = B15 = Marc. X, 17.
24. *Quaedam Opera Rhetorica. char. fol. quibus praeficitur Aesopi Vita. Prolegomena Rhetorices. Aphthonii Progymnasmata. Hermogenes de Inventione. Idem*

de Ideis. Idem de methodo. Characteres Theophrasti. Dionysius Halicarnasseus de Compositione. Libanii Progymnasmata. = B21 = Marc. XI, 2.
25. *Libri VIII Physicorum Aristot. elegantissimè conscripti. f. m.* = B35 = Marc. IV, 4.
26. *Chrysostomi com. in Mattheum, charactere antiquo. f. m.* = B71 = Marc. II, 182.
27. *Eiusdem com. in Genesim antiquissimo charactere. Incipit, εἰς τὴν εἴσοδον τῆς ἁγίας M. &c.* = B70 = Marc. II, 4.
28. *Galenus de Diebus Criticis. Hali auctor ex Indis, apud Graecos Avecianus sonat de orina à barbaro idiomate in linguam Graecam traductus à peritissimo D. Christodulo. Synopsis de Orina ex Indis. Theophilus περὶ διαχωρημάτων. fol. chart.* = B32 = Marc. V, 8.
29. *Euripides fol. ch. cum variis lectionibus.* = B18 = Marc. IX, 11.
30. *Quartus Physicorum Philoponi. fol. ch.* = B40 = Marc. IV, 20.
31. *Quaedam Manuelis Calecae de processione Spiritus Sancti in favorem Latinorum. fol. ch.* = B69 = Marc. II, 16.
32. *Amonii Philosophi in artem veterem. m. f. eleganter scriptus liber.* = A130 = Marc. IV, 12.
33. *Epistolae Phalaridis Tyranni. m. f.* = B14 = Marc. VIII, 11.
34. *Diodori Siculi Libr. XI. usque ad XX. f. m.* = A117 = Marc. VII, 8.
35. *Euripides cum notis. f. m. Fuit Iacobi Semiteculi.* = A157 = Marc. IX, 10.
36. *Iulii Pollucis Onomasticon. Aeschyli Tragoediae duae. Dionysius de Situ Orbis. Theocriti Eclogae. f. ch.* = B12 = Marc. XI, 7.
37. *Ilias Homeri. fol. memb.* = A124 = Marc. IX, 5.
38. *Plutarchi Vitae. fol. m.* = B20 = Marc. IV, 55.
39. *Appianus Alexandrinus. f. m.* = A158 = Marc. VII, 10.
40. *Georgicon diversorum. Idem cum edito Basileae, qui inscribitur Geoponica. Stephanus de Vrbibus. fol. m. eleganter scriptus.* = A152 = Marc. XI, 12.
41. *Apollonii Opera. in 8. m. Fuit Aloysii Bembi Nobilis Veneti.* = A129 = Marc. X, 1.
42. *Aristotelis De Principiis naturalibus. De Partibus Animalium. De Generatione Animalium. De Anima. De Sensu, & Sensato. De Memoria, & reminiscentia. De Motu animalium. De Somno, & vigilia. De Longitudine, & brevitate vitae.* = B47, B48 = Marc. IV, 24.

Pluteus III.

43. *Themistius in Lib. de Anima. f. m.* = B43 = Marc. IV, 13.
44. *Lysiae Vita scripta à Plutarcho, vel, ut aliis placet, à Dionysio Halicarnassaeo. m. 4.* = A139 = Marc. VIII, 1.
45. *Nili Cabasilae Archiepiscopi Thessalonicensis opus de Spiritu Sancto in favorem Latinorum: scilicet quod Spiritus Sanctus procedat ex Filio. De Sacro Oecumenico Concilio. quod constituit in thronorum Constantinopolitanum Fossium [sic, l. Photium] Patriarcham, & destruxit scandala duarum Ecclesiarum novae &*

antiquae Romae. Doctissimus Barlaam de primatu Papae. Is fuit Monachus S. Basilii Calaber, & scripsit contra Latinos. Antiquum scriptum S. Thomae ad quendam Cantorem Antiochenum; quomodo sit intelligenda processio Spiritus Sancti. De causa Incarnationis, Quomodo Verbum factum sit Homo, &c. f. ch. = B64 = Marc. II, 9.

46. *Alexandri Aphrodisaei com. in lib. Analyticorum Arisstotelis. f. c.* = A93 = Marc. IV, 7.
47. *Idem Alex. ad Sophisticos Elenchos. m. fol. Erat Laurentii Prioli Patricii Veneti.* = A123 = Marc. IV, 8.
48. *Idem in IIII Meteorum. f. c.* = B41 = Marc. IV, 6.
49. *Demosthenis Orationes. c. f.* = B10 = Marc. VIII, 3.
50. *Alterum exempl. in m. f.* = B11 = Marc. VIII, 4.
51. *Aristotelis Politica. f. m.* = Marc. IV, 3. This is the first reference to the manuscript on these lists. John Rhosus wrote *Politics* at Rome in May of 1494. Tomasini does not mention the following *Oeconomics* which Rhosus wrote in June of the same year. The first guard leaf has a rare John and Paul *ex libris*, the second guard has what may be that of a private individual, two words I have not read clearly: "Capito. . .i pali..nti." Tomasini saw a twin of this composite (his page 15), surely also by Rhosus, in the nearby library of S. Antonio di Castello: *Libri Politicorum cum Oeconomica Aristotelis transcripti Romae 1494. f.m.* This codex had earlier belonged to Cardinal Domenico Grimani and Giovanni Pico della Mirandola.[3] It seems to have perished in a disastrous fire at S. Antonio in the eighteenth century. How Zanipolo acquired its copy is not known.
52. *Theodori Grammatica. f.* = B26 = Marc. X, 11.
53. *Paraphrasis ad Moralia Arist. Incipit:* ἐν πάσῃ τέχνῃ, *&c.* = B44 = Marc. IV, 21.
54. *Paraphrasis in ultimos libros Ethicorum. Initium:* ἐπεὶ ἐν τοῖς προειρημένοις περὶ τῶν, *&c.* = B45 = Marc. IV, 22.
55. *Platonis definitiones & Epistolae. Item Epistolae Theodori Thessalonicensis Gazae,* περὶ ἑκουσίου, καὶ ἀκουσίου. = B3 = Marc. IV, 2.
56. *Galeni commentaria in Hippocratem. Volumen ingens. ch. f.* = B55, A95, A105 = Marc. V, 9.
57. *Rhetores Graeci. Incipiunt,* τὴν μὲν παρασκευὴν ὦ ἄνδρε καὶ τὴν προθυμίαν, *&c.* = A122 = Marc. VIII, 6.
58. *S. Thomae contra Gentes tertius Liber.* = B72 = Marc. II, 3.
59. *Alterum Exempl. m. 4. Graecè traductum à doctissimo Demetrio Cydonio. Quod in Bibl. Vaticana aspexit Gesnerus.* This must be Marc. II, 2, part 2, with one of Tomasini's frequent errors about material.

---

[3] See Diller, Saffrey, and Westerink, *Bibliotheca Graeca*, 114.

60. *Dionysii Halicarnassaei Methodi Panegyricorum, Epithalamiorum, Epitaphiorum &c. m. f.* = B86 = Marc. VIII, 10.
61. *S. Augustinus de Trinitate. m. f.* = Marc. II, 2, part 1. See number 59 above.
62. *Diodorus Siculus. 4. m.* = A117 = Marc. VII, 7.

Pluteus V. Graeci.

63. *Synesius de Somniis cum commentatio. 4. m.* = B49 = Marc. XI, 9.
64. *Pindari Opera cum Scholiaste, charactere elegantissimo.* = A121 = Marc. IX, 8.
65. *Eustatius de Ismini & Esmeniae fab. m. 4. Herodianus de Caesaribus. m. 4.* = A144. *Dionysius de Structura Orationis & locutione verborum. m. 4.* = A120 = Marc. XI, 14.
66. *Philostrati Imagines, Epigram. m. 4.* = B23 = Marc. XI, 15.
67. *Libanii orationes. 4. m.* = B22 = Marc. VIII, 9.
68. *Theodori περὶ ἑκουσίου, καὶ ἀκουσίου.*
    Anonymi. ὅτι τὰ οὐράνια, &c.
    Georgii Gemisti de Virtute liber ad Regem. De quo Gesnerus.
    Eiusdem πρὸς τὰς τοῦ σχολαρίου ὑπὲρ ἀριστοτέλου ἀτιλίψεις. Πλήθωνος εἰς τὴν βασιλίδα ἑλένη ἐπικήδειος.[4]
    Epistolae Bessarionis ad Gemistum. Incipiunt: Κοινῆς πᾶσιν ἐνεσπαρμένη ἐννοίας καὶ, &c.
    Anonymus. Incipit: πότερα δὲ ὥρισται τε, καὶ ἥμαρται ἅπαντα τὰ μέλλοντα Quod Dictys Cretensis primus scripserit Bellum Troianum: ὅτι ἐπὶ νέρωνος εὑρέθη.. = B90 = Marc. XI, 18.
69. *Basilii, & aliorum Epistolae. Galenus de diebus Criticis. 4. m.* = Marc. XI, 5. See Richter number 10.
70. *Georgii Scholarii Lexicon: περὶ στοιχείων, ἤτοι περὶ γραμμάτων. 4. m.* = B30 = Marc. X, 12.
71. *Pindarus. 4. m.* = A121 = Marc. IX, 9. Tomasini's is the first reference to this manuscript, which came late to the Zanipolo collection. Its origins are obscure. Irigoin[5] has dated the volume to around 1480.

Pluteus VII. Graeci.

72. *Alexandri Aphrodisaei com. in Aristotelis Topica. m. f.* = A132 = Marc. IV, 9.
73. *Thucydidis Historia, charactere antiquo. f. m.* = B7 = Parisinus suppl. gr. 255. See the discussion at B7 and Powell's review.
74. *Alterum Thucydidis exemplar.* = B8 = Marc. VII, 5.

---

[4] Ed. E.V. Maltese, *Georgii Gemisti Plethonis Contra Scholarii pro Aristotele Objectiones* (Leipzig, 1988), V-VIII.

[5] Irigoin, *Histoire du texte de Pindare*, 383.

75. *Moschopulus de Syntaxi. Eiusdem Vocabularium, Psalterium, antiquo & elegantissimo charactere. m. 8.* = B24 = Marc. X, 3.
76. *Arrianus de Alexandri Gestis. Polyaeni stratagemata. Incipit:* τὴν μὲν κατὰ περσῶν, *&c.* = A118 = Marc. VII, 9.
77. *Anonymus. m. fol.* = B77 = Copenhagen Add. 280, 4⁰.
78. *Galenus,* περὶ τῆς τῶν ἁπλῶν φαρμάκων δυνάμεως,, *f. m.* = A 91 = Marc. V, 6.

Zanipolo Manuscripts Acquired Late

Marc. IV, 3— Aristotle *Pol.* and *Oec.* — First reported by Tomasini (51).

Marc. VI, 5— Leo *Tactica* and Choniates — does not appear until Berardelli's catalogue. It is Codex II there and dated to the 15th century. *Repertorium* identifies scribe as John Chonianus (Choniates) from the 16th century.

Marc. VII, 14— Xanthopulus and Codinus — see Vielmi 20.

Marc. IX, 1— Orpheus and Colluthus by Calliergis — This production of Zachary Callierges is first reported by Berardelli, his Codex LXIII.

Marc. IX, 13— *Christus patiens* — does not appear until Berardelli, his Codex LXII. Watermark given by Mioni dates to c. 1535.

Marc. XI, 10— Varia — First reported by Berardelli, his Codex LXXVI. The watermark seems closer to Briquet 7295 than Mioni's 7296, but this has no effect on a date c.1535. Aristobulus Apostolis is the scribe in a non-calligraphic style.

Marc. XI, 11— Onosander, Aelian, etc. — A collection of several originally separate Greek and Latin MSS. Largely by Bartolomeo Zanetti and Camillus Venetus (see Harlfinger, *Textgeschichte*, 299–300). Too late to have appeared on early lists. Listed by Berardelli among Latin texts as item 401.

Concordance of Manuscript References

L = Janus Lascaris
A = Giovanni de Rachaneto
G = Conrad Gesner
T = Filippo Tomasini

B = Gioachino Torriano
R = Martin Richter
V = Girolamo Vielmi

Marc. I, 1 (coll. 1274) —	B 60, T 75
Marc. II, 2 (coll. 1012) —	B 72 (?), T 61
Marc. II, 3 (coll. 1437) —	B 72, T 58 (+ 59 ?)
Marc. II, 4 (coll. 832) —	B 70, R 3, T 27
Marc. II, 9 (coll. 1438) —	B 64, T 45
Marc. II, 16 (coll. 1103) —	B 69, T 31
Marc. II, 182 (coll. 1114) —	B 71, R 8, T 26
Marc. IV, 1 (coll. 542) —	B 1, R 27, T 20
Marc. IV, 2 (coll. 1185) —	B 3, R 100, T 55
Marc. IV, 3 (coll. 1186) —	T 51
Marc. IV, 4 (coll. 1326) —	B 35, R 34, T 25
Marc. IV, 5 (coll. 1003) —	B 5, T 16
Marc. IV, 6 (coll. 1327) —	L 3, B 41, R 40, V 6, T 48
Marc. IV, 7 (coll. 1328) —	A 93, R 58, V 7, T 46
Marc. IV, 8 (coll. 1152) —	A 123, A 128, R 58, T 47
Marc. IV, 9 (coll. 1095) —	A 132, R 58, T 72
Marc. IV, 10 (coll. 833) —	A 126, R 46, V 5, T 15
Marc. IV, 12 (coll. 1115) —	A 130, R 56, T 32
Marc. IV, 13 (coll. 1329) —	L 6, B 43, T 43
Marc. IV, 14 (coll. 935) —	B 34, R 57, T 8
Marc. IV, 15 (coll. 1187) —	B 36, R 36, V 4 & V 32, T 9
Marc. IV, 16 (coll. 1330) —	B 37, R 37, V 4, T 10
Marc. IV, 17 (coll. 1331) —	B 38, R 37, V 4, T 11
Marc. IV, 18 (coll. 1332) —	B 39, R 37, V 4, T 12
Marc. IV, 19 (coll. 1188) —	L 5, B 42, R 43, T 13
Marc. IV, 20 (coll. 1189) —	L 8, B 40, R 35, T 30
Marc. IV, 21 (coll. 1296) —	B 44, R 53, G 7, T 53
Marc. IV, 22 (coll. 1297) —	B 45, R 53, G 7, T 54
Marc. IV, 24 (coll. 1132) —	L 7, B 47 & B 48, R 41, V 27, T 42

Marc. IV, 26 (coll. 1442)—	A 133, R 32, G 16, T 21
Marc. IV, 29 (coll. 1063)—	A 131, R 82, T 6
Marc. IV, 55 (coll. 1191)—	B 20, R 76, V 21, T 38
Marc. V, 4 (coll. 544)—	A 151, R 20, R 21
Marc. V, 5 (coll. 1053)—	A 153, R 14, R 21 , R 22 ?
Marc. V, 6 (coll. 1207)—	A 91 (?), A 105, R 19, T 78
Marc. V, 7 (coll. 1054)—	A 88, R 13,
Marc. V, 8 (coll. 1334)—	B 32, R 17, T 28
Marc. V, 9 (coll. 1017)—	B 55, A 95 & A 105, R 14 & R 16, T 56
Marc. VI, 5 (coll.1065)—	Late acquisition
Marc. VII, 4 (coll. 1155)—	A 119, R 72, T 14
Marc. VII, 5 (coll. 1192)—	B 8, R 74, T 74
Marc. VII, 6 (coll. 1096)—	A 135, R 73, T22
Marc. VII, 7 (coll. 1078)—	A 117, R 77, T 62
Marc. VII, 8 (coll. 1097)—	A 117, R 77, T 34 & T 62
Marc. VII, 9 (coll. 1098)—	A 118, A 159, R 70, T 76
Marc. VII, 10 (coll. 1099)—	A 158, R 71, T 39
Marc. VII, 12 (coll. 1067)—	B 73, R 75, G 6, T 17
Marc. VII, 14 (coll. 568)—	V 20
Marc. VII, 50–	Replacement for Paris. suppl. 255
Marc. VIII, 1 (coll. 1159)—	A 139, R 62, T 44
Marc. VIII, 2 (coll. 1388)—	B 56, R 60, T 4
Marc. VIII, 3 (coll. 1193)—	B 10, R 67, T 49
Marc. VIII, 4 (coll. 1208)—	B 11, R 68, T 50
Marc. VIII, 6 (coll. 1101)—	A 122, R 65, G 19, T 57
Marc. VIII, 7 (coll. 1069)—	B 75, A 148, R 64, T 1
Marc. VIII, 9 (coll. 1038)—	B 22, R 61, T 67
Marc. VIII, 10 (coll. 1349)—	B 86, A 155, R 69, T 60
Marc. VIII, 11 (coll. 1350)—	B 14, R 97, T 33
Marc. VIII, 18 (coll. 1020)—	B 47
Marc. IX, 1 (coll. 1225)—	Late acquisition
Marc. IX, 5 (coll. 1336)—	A 124, R 79, G 1, T 37
Marc. IX, 6 (coll. 1006)—	A 137 & A 159, R 78, G 4, G 14, T 5
Marc. IX, 8 (coll. 1039)—	A 121, R 83, T 64
Marc. IX, 9 (coll. 1181)—	A 121, T 71
Marc. IX, 10 (coll. 1160)—	A 157, R 80, T 35
Marc. IX, 11 (coll. 1196)—	B 18, R 81, T 29
Marc. IX, 12 (coll. 1046)—	B 19, R 80
Marc. IX, 13 (coll. 1470)—	Late acquisition
Marc. IX, 22 (coll. 1161)—	A 104, B 79
Marc. X, 1 (coll. 1374)—	A 129, B 92, R 92, T 41
Marc. X, 2 (coll. 1137)—	B 77

Concordance of Manuscript References

Marc. X, 3 (coll. 1228)—   B 24, R 96, T 75
Marc. X, 5 (coll. 1251)—   B 29, R 95
Marc. X, 6 (coll. 1270)—   B 25, R 94
Marc. X, 11 (coll. 1337)—   B 26, R 93, T 52
Marc. X, 12 (coll. 1139)—   B 27, B 30, T 70
Marc. X, 15 (coll. 1391)—   A 95 & A 106
Marc. X, 17 (coll. 1338)—   B 15, R 86, V 9, T 23
Marc. XI, 1 (coll. 452)—   A 147
Marc. XI, 2 (coll. 1306)—   B 21, R 63, T 24
Marc. XI, 3 (coll. 973)—   A 149, B 89, R 91, T 3
Marc. XI, 4 (coll. 1008)—   A 140 & A 159, R 89, G 3, G 15,
Marc. XI, 5 (coll. 1254)—   R 10, T 69
Marc. XI, 7 (coll. 1340)—   B 12, R 87, T 36
Marc. XI, 8 (coll. 991)—   B 9, R 85, T 2
Marc. XI, 9 (coll. 1232)—   B 49, R 52, T 63
Marc. XI, 10 (coll. 1474)—   Late acquisition
Marc. XI, 11 (coll. 1375)—   Late acquisition
Marc. XI, 12 (coll. 1084)—   A 127 & A 152 & A 159, R 90, T 40
Marc. XI, 13 (coll. 1009)—   A 138, R 47, V 12, T 7
Marc. XI, 14 (coll. 1233)—   B 92, A 120 & A 144, R 84, T 65
Marc. XI, 15 (coll. 1273)—   B 23, R 99, G 13, T 66
Marc. XI, 18 (coll. 1042)—   B 90, R 50, T 68
Berlin fol. 67–   B 91, R 38
Copenhagen Add. 280, 4⁰–   B 77, T 77
Escorial Φ-III-7–   R 22
Florence, Laurentianus 80.25–   A 101, V 18
Geneva 43 (158)—   A 146, R 98
Ambrosianus R 25 sup.–   A 143, B 85, R 30, R 31, G 10 & G 18
Ambrosianus C 253 inf.–   B 58
Montpellier 120–   A 136, R 33, G 17
Naples III–E –37 –   B 74
Paris. 466–   A 141, R 7
Paris. 495–   B 62, R 5
Paris. 1831, pt. 3–   B 82, G 8
Paris. 1832, pt. 2–   B 84
Paris. 1882–   A 134, R 44
Paris. 1910–   L 4, B 58, R 39
Paris. 1921–   B 57, R 45, G 8
Paris. 1937–   B 33,
Paris. 1970–   B 46, R 29
Paris. 2003–   B 6, R 49
Paris. 2058–   R 51

Paris. 2153–	L 1, B 55, A 98, A 99, R 15, R 20, R 42, G 11
Paris. 2352–	B 51, R 23
Paris. 2398–	L 2, B 52
Paris. suppl. 255–	B 7, R 74, T 73
Toledo 98/14–	B 52
Vatican. Barb. 246–	A 156, B 28, R 48, G 12

Index of Greek Authors and Subjects Mentioned on these Lists

Actuarius, L1, (A 99)
Aeschines, B 11, R 60, R 68, T 4
Aeschylus, B 12, R 87, T 36
Aesop, B 76, T 24
Alcibiades, A 155
Alexander of Aphrodisias, L 3, B 41,
  B 84, A 93, A 123, A 126, A128,
  A132, A134, R 40, R 44, R 46, R 58,
  V 5–7, T 15, T 46–48, T 72
Alexander Trallianus, R 16
Ammonius, A 130, R 56, T 32
Andocides, A 122
Andronicus, G 1
Aneochidi, *see* Andocides
aphorisms, A 153
Aphthonius, T 24
Apollonius Dyscolus, R 60, R 92, T 4,
  T 41
Apollonius Rhodius, B 79
Appian, R 71, T 39
Aristides, (B 75), R 64, T 1
Aristotle, L 7, B 4–5, (B33–45), B 75,
  B 78, B 80, B 84–85, B 91, A 92,
  A 102–103, A 132 R 31, R 33–41,
  R 43–44, R 45, R 53, R 55, R 57–58,
  G 7–8, G 17–18, V 4, V 6–7, V 13,
  V 17, V 27–28, T 8–13, T 16, T 25, T
  42–43, T 46–48, T 51, T 53–54, T 68,
  T 72
Arrian, A 118, R 70, T 76
Athanasius, R 88, G 2
Augustine, T 61
Avicenna, T 28

Barlaam, T 45
Basil, B 62, R 5, R 10, V 29, T 69

Bessarion, T 68
Bible, B 67, R 1, G 20, *see also* Gospels,
  Old Testament, Psalms
Blemmydes, Nicephorus, B 28, A 156,
  R 48, G 12
Brutus, B 14

Cabasilas, Nicephorus, T 45
Calecas, Manuel, T 31
Cantacuzenus, John, *see* Joasaph
Cedrenus, George, R 75, G 6, T 17
Chrysostom, John, B 70–71, A 142, R 3,
  R 8, V 2, T 26–27
Clement of Alexandria, R 89, G 3
Cornutus, *see* Phurnutus
Church Councils, T 45
Cydonius, Demetrius, T 59

David, Nicetas, B 33
Demosthenes, B 10 & 11, A 100, R 67–
  68, T 49–50
Dictys Cretensis, T 68
Didymus, A 124
Dio Chrysostom, B 53, R 54, G 5
Diogenes Laertius, V 32
Diodorus Siculus, A 117, R 77, T 34, T 62
Dionysius Halicarnasseus, B 12, B 86,
  A 120, A 135, R 69, R 73, R 84, T 22,
  T 24, T 44, T 60, T 65
Dionysius Periegetes, A 138, R 47, R 87,
  T 7, T 36
Dioscorides, R 17, V 11

Epictetus, R 47, V 12, T 7
epigrams, B 93, R 99, T 66
epistles, T 69

epitaphs, A 95
Eranus, B 77. *See* Zonaras
Euclid, B 51, R 23, R 26, V 8
Euripides, B 18–19, R 80–81, T 29, T 35
Eusebius, B 61, A 6, A12, A 141, R 7, V 23
Eustathius, R 47
Eustathius Macrembolites, R 84, T 65
Eustratius, A 57

Galen, A 5, A 98, A 151, R 12–15, R 17–22, R 42, R 46, T 15, T 28, T 56, T 69, T 78
Gaza, Theodore, B 26, R 50, R 93, T 52, T 55, T 68
geoponica, R 90, T 40
Gospels, B 68, B 71, R 6
grammatica, B 27, B 54, A 129, A 145, R 94–95
Gregory Nazianzenus, R 9
Gregory Nyssenus, V 25

Harpocration, A 146, R 98
Haymon, V 26
Heliodorus, B 44–45, R 53, T 54
Hephestion, R 92
Hermogenes, B 21, R 63, T 24
Herodes, R 65, G 19, T 57
Herodian, A 144, R 84, T 65
Hesiod, B 12, R 78, T 5
Hexaemeron, B 70, R 3, V 25, T 27
Hippocrates, R 14, R 22, T 56
historica, B 73, V 22
Homer, B 74 & 83 & 88, A 124, R 79, G 1, T 37
Horapollo, V 19

Isaiah, B 62, B 66, R 5

Joasaph, G 7
Job, B 65, R 4
John Damascenus, V 31
John grammaticus (Philoponus), L 8, B 40, B 50, B 85, R 24, R 35, R 51, G 8, T 30
Joseph Pinarus Rhacendytes, B 47–48

Julian, A 125, R 66, G 9

Lascaris, Constantine, A 106
lexica, B 13, B 15–17, R 86, R 91, V 1, V 9, T 3, T 23
Libanius, B 22, R 61, T 24, T 67
logica, B 82
Luciano, *see* Lascaris
Lycophron, A 104
Lysias, A 139, R 62, T 44

mathematica, L 2
Maximus Tyrius, A 143, R 30, G 10
medica, A 154, G 8
Metochites, Theodore, B 6, R 49
Michael Ephesius, R 44
Moschion, R 42, G 11
Moschopulus, Manuel, B 24, B 25, B 29, R 95–96, T 75

Nicephorus Callistus Xanthopulus, V 20
Nicomachus Gerasenus, B 50, R 24, R 26, G 8
Nitofano, *see* Lycophron

Old Testament, B 67, R 1, G 20
orina, T 28
Orpheus, B 79

Palaephatus, A 137, R 78
Pappus, B 52
Paul of Tarsus, B 63, V 2–3, V 30
Phalaris, B 14, R 60, R 97, T 4, T 33
Philo Judaeus, V 24
Philopato, *see* Palaephatus
Philoponus, *see* John grammaticus
Philoseno, *see* Syrianus
Philostratus, B 23, R 99, G 13, T 66
Phurnutus, R 78, G 4, G 14
Pindar, A 121, R 83, T 64, T 71
Plato, B 1–3, B 89, R 27–28, R 91, R 100, T 18–20, T 55
Pletho, George Gemistus, R 50, T 68
Plotinus, B 46, R 29

Plutarch, B 20, A 101, R 76, V 18, V 21, T 38, T 44
Polidorus, *see* Polybius
Pollux, B 12, R 87, T 36
Polyaenus, R 70, T 76
Polybius, A 119, R 72, T 14
Polydorus, *see* Pollux
Porphyrius, B 33, A 140, R 29, G 15, V 10, T 16
procession of Holy Spirit, B 64, B 69, T 31, T 45
Proclus Diadochus, B 51, B 81, R 23, R 51
Procopius, R 98
Psalms, B 59–60 & 87, A 94, R 2, G 21, T 75
Ptolemaeus, Claudius, B 52, V 14–15

rhetorica, B 56. R 60, R 65. R 92, G 19, T 24, T 32, T 57

Scholarius, George, B 30, T 68, T 70
Sextus Empiricus, A 133, R 32, G 16, T 21

Simplicius, L 4–5, B 34, B 36, 39, B 42, B 58, R 36–37, R 39, R 43, R 47, R 57, V 4, T 7–13
Soboratus, *see* Sopater
Sopater, R 69
Stephanus Byzantius, A 127, R 90, T 40
Stobaeus, Joannes, A 131, R 82, T 6
Suda, B 9, R 85, T 2
Synesius, B 31, B 49, R 11, R 52, T 63
synodica, T 45
Syrianus Philoxenus, A 136, R 33, G 17, V 13

Themistius, L 6, B 43, T 43
(Themistius), *see* Pletho
Theocritus, B 12, R 87, T 36
Theodoretus, V 3, V 16
Theon, B 52
Theophilus, T 28
Theophrastus, B 57, R 45, T 24
Thomas Aquinas, B 72, T 45, T 58–59
Thucydides, B 7–8, R 74, T 73–74

uroscopy, *see* orina

Verserio, *see* Actuarius

Zonaras, John, B 77

Appendix I

In Chapter IV above it was suggested that in 1494 Gioachino Torriano undertook to continue a project earlier begun by Cardinal Bessarion, namely to create a fine collection of folio-size manuscripts on parchment to serve as the cornerstone for the first public library at Venice. Circumstantial evidence presented there included Torriano's use of scribes whose hands resembled those of Bessarion's scribes and the fact that the start of Torriano's project coincided with his proposal to the Venetian Senate to join the books at San Zanipolo with those of Bessarion. On the chance that this circumstantial evidence is not sufficiently persuasive, it may be well to take a closer look at Bessarion's *pulcherrimi*, especially in the area of duplication by Torriano's *pulcherrimi*, to see if the latter intentionally avoided reproducing texts already in possession of the Venetian Senate in large-format parchment manuscripts. In other words, the point is to see whether Torriano was producing a complementary or an independent collection.

Understanding that Torriano was spending most of his time at Rome as head of the Dominican Order and that, even had he been in Venice, access to Bessarion's books would have been difficult at best, we should assume that any detailed information he had about these books must have been based upon available inventories, such as those provided by Labowsky in her A and B lists.[1] These inventory items must thus be given precedence over the actual state of the manuscripts. Whenever an apparent duplication occurs, a cross-reference to the Bessarion manuscript and that of Torriano is given:

Bessarion *Pulcherrimi*

Marc. gr.			
	5—	B468—	Biblia nova . . .
	6—	A1—	Byblia tota . . .
	B467—	Biblia . . .	

---

[1] Items on this table have been abridged from Labowsky's full transcriptions. Nothing has been omitted, however, that would bear on the question of duplication. Omitted, in addition to unimportant content and description, is the fact that each item is written on parchment—as are many non-*pulcherrimi* in Bessarion's collection. The A and B lists are the only ones known to be available between the time of Bessarion's bequest and 1494.

39—	B505—	Philonis iudei orationes XLVI . . . pulchre.
46—	B506—	Origenes contra Celsum . . .
60—	A158—	S. Basilii expositio in partem Esaiae prophetae . . .
	B196—	S. Basilii in Isaiam . . .
124—	B507—	Cyrilli contra Julianum in defensione evangelii . . .
184—	A411—	Platonis omnia opera . . . pulcher et optimus liber.
	B50—	Omnia opera Platonis in eodem et pulcherrimo volumine . . .
187—	A430—	Platonis respublica, leges et epistolae . . . liber pulcherrimus.
	B525—	Platonis respublica, leges et epistolae . . . SEE MARC. XI, 3
190—	A413—	Procli et Platonici philosophi expositio in Thimaeum Platonis . . . novum et pulcher liber.
	B53—	Proculi in Timeum Platonis . . . novus liber et pulcher.
191—	A414—	Procli Platonici expositio in Parmenidem Platonis . . . novus, pulcherrimus.
	B52—	Proculi in Parmenidem Platonis . . .
192—	A415—	Procli Platonici in theologiam Platonis . . . novus, pulcherrimus.
	B54—	Proculi in theologiam Platonis . . . liber novus et pulcher.
193—	A427—	Procli Platonici super theologia Platonis libri duo . . .
	B60—	Proculi duo libri de theologia Platonis . . .
198—	B536—	Opus domini Rev. in calumniatorem Platonis . . .
200—	A359—	Liber novus et pulcherrimus . . . omnia opera Arist. praeter logicam.
	B1—	Totus Aristotelis praeter logicam . . . novus.
206—	B550—	Aristotelis physica cum paraphrasi Themistii . . .
207—	B553—	Aristotelis de historia, et generatione . . . novus.
213—	B554—	Aristotelis ethica magna, nicomachi, eudemia . . . pulcher et novus.
215—	B555—	Aristotelis de arte rhetorica ad Alexandrum . . . novus et pulcher.
219—	A360—	Simplicii . . . expositio in libros physicorum Aristotelis . . . novus liber.
	B2—	Physica Aristotelis cum expositione . . . liber pulcher.
222—	B560—	Simplicii expositio super de caelo . . . liber pulcher . . .
223—	A394—	Philoponi grammatici expositio super de generatione et corruptione . . .

	B6—	Philoponus in librum de generatione et corruptione...
234—	A391—	93— Porphyrii... in praedicamenta... Adamantii...
	B26—	Porphyrii dialogus in praedicamenta Aristotelis...
238—	B558—	Expositiones in de progressu animalium...
243—	A417—	Iamblici Chalcidiensis de secta Pythagorae... liber novus, pulcher.
	B57—	Iamblici de secta Pythagorae...
245—	A423—	Damaskii... quaestiones de primis principiis... novus.
	B59—	Damasceni de principiis in Parmenidem...
248—	A412—	Plutarchi moralia, physica, politica... novo et pulcherrimo.
	B51—	Omnia moralia Plutarchi...
253—	B532—	Ariani de dictis Epictheti... Simplicii expositio in enchiridion eiusdem Epictheti, et Eustachii in primo moralium nicomacheorum... SEE MARC. XI, 13
254—	A424—	Maximi Tyrii sophistae quid est deus secundum Platonem, et alia eius opera... SEE AMBROS. R 25 sup.
	B24—	Maximi Platonici orationes...
262—	A408—	Sexti akademici philosophi...
	B616—	Sextus academaicus... SEE MARC. IV, 26
263—	A426—	Liber in pergameno, novus, pulcher... incipit a mechanicis Heronis et finit in Ephestionem de metris.
	B644—	Liber... incipit a mechanicis Heronis et finit in Ephestionem de metris... pulcher. SEE MARC. X, 1
267–68—	B620—	21— Artemidori de iudiciis insomniorum...
270—	B661—	Aretei de causis et signis passionum acutarum...
272—	A218—	Dioscurides medicus...
274—	A400—	Theophrasti philosophi de historia et generatione plantarum...
	B5—	Theophrastus de plantis...
275—	A206—	Galieni microthechnae et alia multa...[2]
	B653—	Galieni microtechnica [et alia multa]
279—	B655—	Galieni de anatomia [et alia multa]... novum opus.

---

[2] These Galen items, Marc. gr. 275 to 287, are the subject of a separate Appendix which follows.

280—	B656—	Galieni ad Glauconem therapeuticae parvae . . . .
281—	B664—	Galieni commentum in librum Hypocratis de acutis aegritudinibus . . .
282—	B659—	Galieni de cena pueri epileptici . . . novus.
284—	B660—	Galieni de dogmatibus Hypocratis et Platonis . . . novus.
285—	B657—	Galieni in aphorismos Hypocratis . . . novus.
286—	B654—	Galieni de simplicibus farmacis libri XI . . .
287—	B658—	Galieni de utilitate membrorum humani corporis . . . novus.
289—	A204—	Aetii medici medietas libri . . .
	B651—	Aetii prima medietas . . .
290—	B652—	Aetii secunda medietas . . .
293—	A203—	Alter Paulus Aeginites . . . novus.
	B133—	Pauli Eginete medici . . .
298—	B666—	Opera Octuarii . . .
305—	A261—	Archimedis diversa opera geometrica, et Eutocii in Archimedem . . .
	B586—	Archimedis diversa opera geometrica cum expositione Eustochii . . .
322—	B571—	Liber musicae novus . . . liber optimus . . . et difficilis inventu.
337—	A197—	Historiae ecclesiasticae, vz. Eusebius Pamphili . . . novus et pulcher liber.
	B477—	Historiae ecclesiasticae Eusebii, Theodorici, Socratis . . .
342—	B503—	Eusebii Pamphili evangelica praeparatio . . . SEE PARIS. 466
345—	A45—	Theodoriti orationes monasticae et Palladii ad Lausum . . .
	B273—	Sanctorum patrum vitae per Theodoretum Ciri et Palladium . . .
364—	B607—	Heroditi, Thucidydis, et Xenophontis historiae . . . novus liber.
369—	B608—	Xenophontis de institutione Cyri maioris . . . novus liber.
373—	B605—	Dionisii Halicarnasei de romana antiquitate . . . novus. SEE MARC. VII, 6
378—	B604—	Strabonis totum opus . . . novum.
380—	B601—	Josephi de iudaica antiquitate . . . novus.
384—	A315—	Plutarchi vitae, sive paralleli . . . liber novus, pulcherrimus.
	B79—	Plutarchi paralella omnia, liber pulcherrimus.

388—	A243—	Ptolemei geographia, depicta, pulcherrima, in magno volumine ...
	B462—	Ptolomei geographia pulcherrima graece cum picturis ...
390—	A350—	Herodianus historicus de octo caesaribus, et Sosimus ...
	B30—	Herodiani de octo caesaribus, et Sosini historici ... SEE MARC. XI, 14
392—	B597—	Philostrati vitae sophistarum ... novus.
394—	A349—	Diogenes Laertius de vitis philosophorum ...
	B28—	Laertii Diogenis de vita philosophorum ...
396—	A320—	Dionis Romanarum historiarum ...
	B72—	Dionis romanarum historiarum ...
397—	A343—	Historia de rebus gestis Mauritii ... et Asclepii Traiani ...
	B61—	Historia de rebus gestis Mauricii ... et Esculapii Tralani ...
405—	A344—	Nicephori Gregorae historia ...
	B62—	Niciphori Grigorii ...
413—	A388—	Pausaniae descriptio Graeciae, et Simplicius ...
	B543—	Descriptio graeciae per Pausaniam, et Simplicii de anima ...
414—	A346—	Polyaeni strategemata ...
	B619—	Polieni stratagemata ... SEE MARC. VII, 9
415—	A306—	Isocratis oratoris orationes ... Dionysii de compositione nominum.
	B80—	Isocratis orationes ... Dionisii de nominum compositione. SEE MARC. XI, 14
421—	A302—	Dionis Chrysostomi orationes ...
	B85—	Dionis Chrysostomi orationes ...
429—	A305—	Multa et pulchra de arte rhetorica ... a Dionysio Alicarnasseo ... in Minucianum de argumentationibus.
	B86—	Dionisii Alicarnasei, Demetrii Phalerensis, Alexandri, Menandri, Aristidis, Hapsyni, Minuciani oratorum multa et pulchra de ratione dicendi. SEE MARC. VIII, 10
435—	B606—	Luciani omnia opera ... nova.
449—	B680—	Suida ...
456—	A443—	Homeri Ilias, et Quinti poetae ... liber novus, optimus ...

	B37—	Homeri ilias, odyssea . . . Quinti supplementum . . .
461—	62 —	A448— 449— Eustathii expositio in . . . libros iliadis Homeri . . .
	B41—42—	Heustachii in . . . libros iliadis . . .
470—	B635—	Euripidis tragoediae . . . Sophoclis . . . Aeschyli . . . pulchro.
475—	B636—	Aristophanis comoediae . . . Pindari . . . Lycophron . . . novus et pulcher . . . SEE MARC. IX, 8
480—	B639—	Oppiani de piscibus et venatione, Theocriti eglogae, Dionisii cosmographia . . . Nicandri thiriaca et alexipharmaca, Aglai quoddam . . . Arati phenomena . . . Hesiodi omnia . . . Apollonii argonautica, Orphei argonautica et hymni, Callimachi hymni . . . novus et pulcher . . . SEE MARC. XI, 13
518—	A242—	Heliani de proprietatibus animalium, Eunapii . . .
	B585—	Heliani de proprietatibus animalium, Eunapii . . .
522—	A304—	Lisias orator, Agathii historia, Theognus . . .
	B83—	Lisiae orationes, Dionisii de charactere Lisiae, Gorgiae . . . Adamantis . . . Antistenis . . . Demadis . . . Agathis . . .

SEE MARC. VIII, 1, VIII, 2, and VIII, 6

Leaving aside for the moment the Galen items on the list above, a subject treated separately in Appendix II, there are in the 71 remaining items 14 instances of duplication (Marc. 187, 253, 254, 262, 263, 342, 373, 390, 414, 415, 429, 475, 480, and 522). This is a significant number, but if Torriano depended upon available inventories for his familiarity with Bessarion's library, not searching through packing cases, the duplications can be better understood. Items which refer to the "beauty" of the volume in their descriptions would have sent a warning signal against duplication to Torriano. He seems to have generally avoided including such items among his own *pulcherrimi*. On the Bessarion list above there are eighteen items which include various forms of the word *pulcher* in their descriptions and there are 10 others elsewhere in the A and B lists (Marc. 8, 17, 104, 111, 108, 113, 143, 416, 453, the unidentified item at A 85–B472). Of those twenty-eight only five could be considered Torriano duplications, that is, manuscripts the inventory descriptions of which warn that the item may fall into the category of the *pulcherrimi*. These five require special attention:

Marc. 187— It is not clear whether Torriano used Labowsky's A or B list, or both. But the B list does not use the adjective *pulcher* found in the A list description. Of the three works contained in Bessarion's codex, only *Laws* appears in Marc. XI, 3. This *pulcherrimus* was among the first produced for Torriano, in any case, and it appears that he had a definite reason for producing it early and separately from other works of Plato.

Marc. 263 — The message of both the A and B lists for this item is that many works were included here and that Hephestion ended the run of materials. Perhaps Torriano had a reason for creating a metrics text separate from the rest. Failure to use a superlative of *pulcher* in the description may also play a part here. One must also consider the difficulty in singling out authors for copying without an alphabetic master list. Some duplication was almost unavoidable with the A and B inventories as a reference source.

Marc. 429 — The word *pulchra* used here modifies the "many things" in the codex and does not refer to the codex itself. Bessarion elsewhere refers to *pulchrae orationes* (Marc. 108, 111, 113) in manuscripts which were not *pulcherrimi*. Torriano must be excused for not recognizing one here.

Marc. 475 — Pindar is here surrounded by other works. In Marc. IX, 8 *Olympians* and *Pythians* are repeated, but the main part of the manuscript is a separate section of scholia on the odes, not found in Marc. 475 and requiring an associated text here.

Marc. 480 — Dionysius Periegetes, often called Dionysius Alexandrinus in the manuscripts, is not differentiated on Labowsky's B list with a helpful epithet so as to distinguish him from others of the same name. Nor does *cosmographia* in any way help in recognizing his poem. If this was an unconscious duplication, there is surely sufficient reason for it.

Torriano's avoidance of authors and texts represented in Bessarion's *pulcherrimi* is therefore marked and clear. His own *pulcherrimi* were to be a complement to those of the cardinal, featuring works which would at the same time enhance both the collection he had been putting together for over a decade and that of Cardinal Bessarion.

Appendix II

Marcianus V, 4 and V, 5 must be treated independently of other manuscripts and other *pulcherrimi* when dealing with the matter of duplication of contents. First of all, they contain a large number of works, long and short, of Galen. Avoiding repetition of works found in manuscripts of Cardinal Bessarion would be a difficult and involved task which probably went beyond the efforts Caesar Strategus, the scribe of both Marc. V, 4 and V, 5, was prepared to offer. His limited care is obvious when we find in Marc. V, 5 the treatise *De atra bile* at folio 322 repeated at folio 416. He did the same with *De purgantium facultate* in Marc. V, 4 and V, 5. If Strategus could make such inadvertent repetitions in manuscripts immediately before him, how easy would it have been to duplicate opuscula of Galen included in Bessarion manuscripts at some distance from his activity? A second reason for some repetitions will be offered below in the reconstruction of the exemplar used by Strategus.

As was shown above at Marcon numbers A 151 and 153, Marc. V, 4 and V, 5 consist of three parts distinguished by independent quire signatures which have today been bound into two volumes. All three parts were written at a time too late to be entered on his B list by Torriano (d. 1500), but soon enough for de Rachaneto to have seen them in the early years of the sixteenth century. The sequence of presentation of Galen's works in the two codices, in whatever order the three sections are placed, is so unusual when compared with other manuscripts of similar content that we cannot help suspecting that the exemplar used by Strategus was unbound and that the scribe was free to jump around from an opusculum ending one quire to any other beginning another quire. The mutilated state of many opuscula points also to the likelihood that several quires were incomplete, another mark of an unbound codex.

Guidorizzi has made an interesting observation about the opusculum *De dignotione ex insomniis* in Marc. V, 5.[1] After placing the manuscript (M) into a small group of witnesses (his b family) and a smaller subgroup with Modena 213 (Q) and Leyden Voss. Q 45 (N), Guidorizzi says: "... nessuno di questi tre codici è la fonte degli altri e ... dipendono tutti da un unico esemplare, ora perduto"

---

[1] G. Guidorizzi, "L'opusculo di Galeno *De dignotione ex insomniis*," *Bollettino del Comitato per la Preparazione dell'Edizione Nazionale dei Classici Greci e Latini* n.s. 21 (1973): 81–105, here 82, 87.

(87). There are seven other contiguous works of Galen in the Modena codex.² All but one are found also between folios 328 and 416 of Marc. V, 5 in an order different from that of the Modena codex. The one work not found in Marc. V, 5, *Introductio-Medicus*, the last of the Modena Galen texts, may be a copy of Marc. V, 9. If it is, the Modena manuscript, a selection of texts made for Giorgio Valla (d. 1500), was probably carried out in the library of San Zanipolo from the exemplar of Marc. V, 4 and V, 5, two *pulcherrimi* which would not have been available for use yet. This exemplar would then be the unbound parchment codex listed at A 5 and said to be one containing all the works of Galen. Valla, living at Venice, would have had easy access to such an exemplar.

Guidorizzi's statement that the exemplar itself no longer exists is fortified by the fact that Marc. V, 4 contains four opuscula of Galen: *De victus ratione ex Hippocrate, An in arteriis natura sanguis contineatur, De instrumento odoratus,* and *Adversus Lycum,* works which occur in no other fifteenth-century or older manuscript. The Zanipolo exemplar has not been identified in this study either, but it would not be surprising to find parts of it still in existence. Study of the origins of other works of Galen among the *pulcherrimi* opuscula would be instructive.

Little is known about the history of Vossianus Q 45.³ It appears to be roughly contemporaneous with codices M and Q. Its quire numbers indicate that the volume once contained many more works than are now present. Those which remain are six in number, the last four being found also between folios 330v and 334v in Marc. V, 5, but in an order different from that of both M and Q. The first two opuscula are found in Marc. V, 4 on folios 278 to 288v. These data indicate that the Leiden manuscript at one time bore many more similarities to the Marciani and was written at Venice late in the fifteenth century from an unbound and disordered exemplar.

The two Marciani *pulcherrimi* have been shown therefore to be essentially a replacement for an older, unbound, and deteriorating manuscript which had been part of the San Zanipolo library before Gioachino Torriano began his ambitious plan to turn it into the municipal library of San Marco. Reproduction of the faulty codex seems then to have taken precedence over the need to avoid duplication of a few works found also among the sequestered manuscripts of Cardinal Bessarion. When the *pulcherrimi* were eventually bound, the older volume(s) apparently became expendable.

---

[2] V. Puntoni, "Indice dei codici greci della Biblioteca Estense di Modena," *Studi italiani di filologia classica* 4 (1896): 379–536, here 509.

[3] K.A. De Meyier, *Leyden, Rijksuniversiteit Bibliothek, Codices manuscripti VI: Codices Vossiani Graeci et Miscellanei* (Leyden, 1955).